CANADA
IN CHAOS

CANADA IN CHAOS

ENERGY EXCELLENCE,
CLIMATE HYSTERIA AND
COVID CATASTROPHE

WALTER BENSTEAD

LitPrime Solutions
21250 Hawthorne Blvd
Suite 500, Torrance, CA 90503
www.litprime.com
Phone: 1 (209) 788-3500

© 2020 Walter Benstead. All rights reserved.

No part of this book may be reproduced, stored in a retrieval system, or transmitted by any means without the written permission of the author.

Published by LitPrime Solutions   12/17/2020

ISBN: 978-1-953397-51-5(sc)
ISBN: 978-1-953397-52-2(hc)
ISBN: 978-1-953397-50-8(e)

Any people depicted in stock imagery provided by iStock are models, and such images are being used for illustrative purposes only.

Certain stock imagery © iStock.

Because of the dynamic nature of the Internet, any web addresses or links contained in this book may have changed since publication and may no longer be valid. The views expressed in this work are solely those of the author and do not necessarily reflect the views of the publisher, and the publisher hereby disclaims any responsibility for them.

CONTENTS

Introduction ix

Chapter 1	Mackenzie Valley Pipeline and Northern Exploration 1
Chapter 2	Politics, Disaster and the National Energy Program 7
Chapter 3	Bilingualism 13
Chapter 4	Better Politics and Movement Forward 17
Chapter 5	Northern Gateway Pipeline 31
Chapter 6	Miscellaneous Issues and Events 45
Chapter 7	Climate Change 57
Chapter 8	Political Disaster Returns 83
Chapter 9	Indigenous Issues 101
Chapter 10	Trans Mountain Pipeline and Expansion Program 113
Chapter 11	Covid 19 Addendum 129

Bibliography 141

PREFACE

This book was originally written about the poor economic decisions of the Canadian government and judicial games that destroyed a vibrant oil and gas industry. The book outlines the efforts, dreams and courageous innovation that built a base framework of the economy for Canada and indeed North America. It describes how proposed resource development brought opportunity to Indigenous people. The stance of media and government opposed rather than supported this. The fallacy of the Climate Hysteria that was used to destroy movement forward is exposed in detail. More solid economic approaches were suggested. The advent of Covid 19 has been a serious medical issue BUT much worse is how it has been used by government to swamp all sense of socioeconomic reality both in the past and for a future recovery. Talk is of a Great Reset. Do not let dictatorship and United Nations based socialism replace the Free Enterprise System that built and sustains North America.

INTRODUCTION

The age of fossil fuels is not over. If you rigidly disagree with that statement, this book is not for you. Resource development has been a backbone of our domestic economy for the past hundred years. Our oil and gas industry has been a major part of that. Canadian expertise and ingenuity in resource development has also had a significant international component. Our current oil and gas industry has been strangled by misplaced bureaucracy, and its free enterprise spirit and prosperity is being squandered. Solar, wind and biofuel powers have failed to meet unrealistic expectations. Today's standard of living is based on oil and gas consumption, as much as the popular media and government wish to deny it.

Canadians have a strong work ethic. They are among the most industrious people in the world. This may partly come from the background of those who built the great British Empire in North America and around the world. It comes from the *coureur des bois* ("runners of the woods"), who paddled from Montreal up the Great Lakes and rivers to tame the west. It comes from the Ukrainian settlers who escaped Russian oppression and valiantly struggled to eke a subsistence living out of a harsh prairie landscape. It comes from the Irish who escaped the potato famine, came to Canada and worked heart and soul to survive. It comes from Americans who came to tame a second frontier.

Mostly, I think, it comes from the land. Canada is a vast and cold country. There is a necessity to confront and conquer the elements. Motivation is established in the fight for survival and continues to drive us to achieve great things. The more we move from the land, the more we urbanize, this somewhat weakens the premise. The essence of the motivation and drive carries on.

The Canadian work ethic is and has been supported by a world-class educational system. Universities such as Dalhousie in Halifax, McGill in Montreal, Western in Toronto and Queens in Ontario are a prestigious base. They provided to Canada and the world scientists, engineers, medical doctors, authors and poets. The Ontario Agricultural College, now the University of Guelph, is an international pillar of agricultural and veterinary science. The western educational base grew from universities of Manitoba, Saskatchewan, Alberta and British Columbia. There are now 10 times as many universities and colleges, all with significant standards. The basic literacy rate in Canada has been one of the highest in the world although today's educational system seems to focus more on brainwashing rather than independent thinking.

Sitting beside the United States, we have had access to major capital and financial resources. Our five major banks, the Royal, CIBC, the Toronto-Dominion, Bank of Nova Scotia and the Bank of Montreal, were and are world-class institutions both domestically and abroad. During the Second World War, Canada was a major player. This smaller nation of 25 million had the fourth-largest military organization in the world. From Dieppe and Sicily to the D-Day landings at Normandy, Canada was one of the world's great middle powers. This was the basis for a proud and prosperous Canada. Prime Minister Sir Wilfrid Laurier proclaimed the 20th century belonged to Canada.

The development of our vast natural resources has fuelled a government-funded national healthcare system, affordable housing and a world-class educational system. The less fortunate are supported by the government.

Our free enterprise system has provided opportunity and prosperity, but now that prosperity is in peril. Development and opportunities are stalled.

In the ongoing chapters, I will discuss three major pipeline infrastructure projects that exemplify this Canadian tragedy: the Mackenzie Valley Pipeline,

Northern Gateway and the Trans Mountain Expansion. All three involved extensive background exploration and development efforts. Regrettably it was mostly spinning wheels and wasted effort. All three projects were stalled by endless delays, judicial blockages and bureaucratic bungling. I was involved in that background for all three. From surface geological mapping to prospect evaluation to drill site supervision I was part of the extensive input effort that went nowhere.

A major background problem in Canada today is the "the noble idea." They are equalization, bilingualism, the National Energy Program, Indigenous Rights and Climate Change pre-occupation. These will be discussed throughout the book. All sounded good. Their ultimate result has been counterproductive bureaucracy and centralization of power.

Resource development in general has a three- to four-year lead time. The demand for and approval or disapproval of the needed product is much more immediate and fickle. There is an initial geological exploration phase—surface or and subsurface geology. I started my career doing surface geology in the high arctic. It was exhilarating and demanding. The observation and compilation of the earth's structures and building blocks gives a detailed picture of the magnificence of God's creation and our natural surroundings. The majesty of hundreds of millions of years of sedimentation, their layering, compression and subsequent twisting and folding is a real story more exciting than any adventure novel. There are 15,000 plus wells drilled in Western Canada and the Northwest Territories. Each has a story to tell. It is documented by drill cuttings and cores as the wells are drilling. At the end of drilling down hole electrical, sonic and porosity surveys referred to as logs are ran. All of this is on file at provincial government well monitoring facilities. Go take a look and see a piece of the earth 1000m below you. Subsurface geology puts together the puzzle from existing wellbores. Connecting individual wells outlines the layering of the earth or "stratigraphy". This can be used to delineate zones, further development and monitor the non-contamination of groundwater.

The second stage is mineral rights acquisition. These could from the government, indigenous band governments, private ownership or other entities.

The third stage is seismic surveys and geophysical evaluation. Compilation and evaluation lead to selecting drilling locations.

The fourth phase is the actual drilling.

The fifth phase is testing and establishing production facilities.

In summary, the phases are as follows:

1. Geological Exploration
2. Mineral Rights Acquisition
3. Geophysical Evaluation
4. Drilling
5. Production Facilities

If you emphatically believe the oil and gas industry is intrinsically evil, this book is not for you. If you believe that it consists of conscientious people and organizations working hard to provide a needed product, then read away. Listen to the problems of the Canadian industry and help us get things back on track. I worked with pride in the industry for 40 years. It is a matter of doing things the right way, not dogmatically blocking all development.

The industry that I loved and the prosperity it brought to Canada are in peril. So much effort by so many has been wasted. I hope my book will be a guide to help steer us back in the right direction.

CHAPTER 1

Mackenzie Valley Pipeline and Northern Exploration

The quest for resource development in the far north was embarked upon as a major element needed to solidify Canadian claims to the Arctic Archipelago. Reconnaissance fieldwork by the Geological Survey of Canada was started in 1954 and continued through 1955, 1958 and 1959. The background facilitation for this was aerial photography started as early as 1950. No satellite photos in those years. The Canadian Arctic Islands have little or no forestry or vegetation coverage, so it has complete exposure of the surface geological framework of the area. The sequence involves some 20,000 feet of sedimentary rock, ranging from the Palaeozoic Era some 250–400 million years ago through the Cretaceous period some 65–150 million years ago to the Tertiary period about 2.5–65 million years ago.

As a student geologist at that time, I was more mind-blown and educated by this geological panorama than any textbook or professor. Exposed on Melville Island were major anticlines with thousand-foot shale sandstone sequences. These were the classical geological setting for major oilfields. All the components were there source rock, reservoir and structural traps. Other classic geological hydrocarbon potential was indicated by Palaeozoic Reefs on Bathurst Island and diapir intrusions on the Sabine Peninsula. I recall an actual oil seep on Axel Heiberg Island. Early wells were drilled at Winter Harbour on Melville Island and Bent Horn on Bathurst Island. Oil from the Bent Horn well was actually used in a trial run at a Quebec refinery.

One of the earlier monumental publications on the geology and resource potential of this truly exciting region was the 1964 Geological Survey of Canada publication regarding Melville and Bathurst Islands.[1] I give big credit to what these pioneers accomplished. A significant portion was actually done using dogsleds. The oil industry, running with this significant potential, chose to further explore it. British Petroleum, the French national enterprise and American partner Mobil took

---

[1] Edward T. Tozer and R. Thorsteinsson, *Western Queen Elizabeth Islands, Arctic Archipelago* (Department of Mines and Technical Services, Canada, 1964).

active roles in the detailed surface geological evaluation of the vast potential.

The Canadian Society of Petroleum Geologists published *Future Petroleum Provinces of Canada, Their Geology and Potential—Memoir 1, 1973,* by R. G. McCrossan. At the time, it was a landmark presentation of the state of hydrocarbon resource development and its potential in Canada. It extended across the country from the East Coast, through the historic Ontario Michigan Basin[2] to Hudson Bay, to the North, across Alberta Saskatchewan and through interior British Columbia to the West Coast.

One of the most exciting papers in that publication was on the geology and vast potential of the Canadian Arctic Archipelago. This paper by Ken Drummond, "The Canadian Arctic Islands," described one of the greatest geology-based unexplored sedimentary basins in the world. Drummond conducted surface and subsurface geological exploration work for Mobil Oil Canada for decades across Western Canada and the Arctic. He went on to be a research specialist with the Arctic Institute at a American Ivy League Universty. His most significant contribution still has to be his summary discussion of Arctic Islands' geology and petroleum potential.

The time came, however, to look not at geology and exploration but logistics. Far north development of

---

[2] Ken Drummond, *Arctic Islands in Future Petroleum Provinces of Canada* (Canadian Society of Petroleum Geologists, 1973).

resources had to focus on possible routes to market. The choices were the eastern or western Arctic. The great geological potential of the central and northern Arctic had to be postponed. The eastern Arctic did not have enough documented potential. The immense potential of the 10,000-plus feet of Tertiary and Cretaceous sediments in the Mackenzie Delta and the Beaufort Sea became the focus.

In the early 1970s, Imperial Oil, and to a lesser extent Chevron and others, drilled 10 to 12 very expensive wells in the Mackenzie Delta onshore and near shore. The nearshore wells utilized drilling from artificial islands. This was mostly a Canadian innovation. It seemed better suited to the local shallow water and Arctic ice conditions problems than conventional offshore drilling platforms. The northern towns of Tuktoyaktuk and Inuvik saw a degree of prosperity and economic activity never before seen in the far north Canadian towns. Gas rates and potential reserves were proven phenomenal. Well test rates were in 10–20 MMCFD (million cubic feet per day). Potential reserves were calculated at not only hundreds of billions of cubic feet (BCF) of natural gas but multiple trillions of cubic feet (TCF) per well. The time came to get the product to market. Automatic progress was not as forthcoming as the exploration and development of the potential. Prime Minister Pierre Trudeau and Justice Thomas Burger entered the picture.

The Mackenzie Valley Pipeline inquiry was

commissioned by the Trudeau Liberal government of Canada in March 1974.³ The known socialist antidevelopment Justice Thomas Berger, former leader of British Columbia's New Democratic Party, was appointed to conduct the inquiry. This was after multiple years of drilling and development by Imperial Oil and others in the Mackenzie Delta. Billions to trillions of cubic feet of proven gas reserves had been established in at least a half dozen very expensive wells. Ongoing new threshold wells were being drilled in the offshore Beaufort Sea. This was to be the onset of world-scale hydrocarbon development. Even in the early drilling stages, the previously ignored isolated towns of Inuvik and Tuktoyaktuk were booming. Prosperity was coming to the north.

The inquiry, which cost $5.3 million, involved some 40,000 pages of text and evidence in some 283 volumes was to investigate the social, environmental and economic impact of such a pipeline. The mass of paper required filled a DC-3 aircraft that was required to transport the inquiry around the vast Arctic.

The decision of the inquiry was released in 1977. After four years of extensive research, widespread consultation and mountains of data, the wondrous decision made was that the pipeline should be delayed for 10 years. This type of decision was almost to be expected by the fact that Mr. Trudeau had selected

---

³ Indigenous Foundation, Berger Inquiry, https://indigenousfoundations.arts.ubc.ca/berger_inquiry/.

him. This outcome effectively killed future drilling and economic activity in the region. It was the first of multiple projects to fall to the great Canadian philosophy of prosperity thwarted by political peril.

CHAPTER 2

Politics, Disaster and the National Energy Program

In the late 1960s and early '70s, something happened or at least began to change. Pierre Trudeau was elected prime minister of Canada and held this position of power from 1968 to 1979. There was a brief respite, and then he regained power from 1980 to 1984. I am not sure whether he led the change or the times had changed and he took advantage of it. Canada, like Europe and the United States, had gone through a period of post war boom. The war was over, and the emphasis was on trying to rebuild the domestic economy. The Western Canadian energy industry was a major part of this.

With Trudeau Senior came a shift from the post war economic reality and productivity to ideas, concepts and wonderful thoughts. Some of these were truly fine and some were not. He was charming, he was fun and he had a certain flair. Canadians had forgotten the war, and although the economic rebuild was flourishing, those not directly involved were bored. Among the most significant of Trudeau's policies was bilingualism, which we will discuss further in chapter 4.

Let us now look at what was probably the second-worst legislation of the Senior Trudeau administration: the NEP (National Energy Program).

In 1980, the NEP was an attempt by the Trudeau Government to gain control over the then free enterprise Canadian petroleum industry. It may well have been US dominated (what the heck? it was free enterprise and not billed to the Canadian taxpayer or controlled from 3,000 kilometres away).

The next socialist idealization factor was that Alberta oil revenue (i.e., funds from an area that was doing something) could be redistributed to other parts of the country. This was an aspect of the chronic "virtue signalling" that both Trudeaus indulged in. Sharing with others? What a wonderful concept. But it wasn't. It weakened areas of productivity. It encouraged areas of lesser activity to be complacent in their bureaucracy. Mostly it shifted power from the regions to the Trudeau central bureaucracy.

World oil supplies had been tightening as Iran and others in the Middle East had been having disputes and production problems. That petroleum source was becoming risky and potentially very expensive. The merits of Western Canadian oil production had been snubbed by the old money Eastern elite during its exploration and development. It began to take on some previously ignored importance. Much of Western Canadian oil production at that time had a high value and was being shipped mostly to the United States, Sarnia Ontario and, to a lesser extent, Montreal Quebec, refineries.

With the fear of world oil supply restrictions, Trudeau and the background Quebec Laurentian elite made a decision. This was the National Energy Program (NEP) by which a previously ignored Western Canadian petroleum industry would now subsidize Quebec. The Trudeau family's loyalty to Middle East despots seemed to be momentarily expendable.

This was one of the first of the many Liberal government's fruitless attempts to interfere in the economy to artificially support Quebec. The NEP established a forced domestic price of crude oil in the vicinity of $35 per barrel. The world price at the time was escalating to double that or more. Oil exported from Western Canada to the United States or any overseas destination would receive the higher world price. However, the large difference between the artificial domestic $35 price would go to the federal Liberal government. These funds would then be given to Quebec and the Maritime refiners to compensate them for the higher world price and bring the cost of crude oil to their refineries down to an artificial domestic price of $35. Again we saw the power shift from the regions to a Quebec-biased central government. Productivity shifted to bureaucracy masked as a noble cause. Prosperity in peril.

This was the Quebec reward for bad, unpatriotic, judgmental bias of choosing foreign suppliers over supporting Canadian industry. The practice continues to this day. The large crude oil subsidy was passed on to Quebec consumers of retail gasoline. On the other side of the equation, this resulted in billions of dollars of revenue theft from producers in Alberta and to a lesser extent Saskatchewan, Manitoba and British Columbia. The loss and theft were via lost royalties, lost taxes and economic downturn. The economic loss was passed on to the average Western Canadian businesses and residents. Western Canadian citizens, industry and politicians were outraged.

This unilateral attempt by unproductive Ottawa to interfere in the productive economy of free enterprise Western Canada had three supposed objectives. First was to reduce the dependence of Canada on foreign oil. Second was to redistribute, via taxes and royalties, the produced oil wealth of Alberta to the unproductive Ottawa bureaucracy. Third was to increase Canadian ownership in the energy industry.

In the good socialist approach, grants were invoked to elaborate on the program objectives and to supposedly compensate for the thwarted economic activity resulting from the program and the immense regulation. These were called PIP (Petroleum Incentive Program) grants. A massive bureaucracy was created to run them. I and many others participated out of need to have some revenue.

One supposed objective was to promote drilling in frontier areas. This was preached as northern development. The background petty economic thought was that if hydrocarbon production could be established in the Territories, Ottawa would receive the royalties, not the Provinces. There would be an arbitrated 25% federal ownership of northern and offshore oil discoveries.

Let us now return to the discussion of Canada's productivity in political peril.

1. Reduce dependency on foreign oil. The federal government allowed Quebec and the Maritimes to avoid the negative aspects of foreign oil dependency by bailing them out. Hence, in the long term they would and did return to that emphasis. During the world oil crisis, a pipeline was built to carry Western Canadian crude oil from Sarnia to Montreal. It was subsequently reversed to carry foreign oil to Sarnia. Oil and gas development in Western Canada was dampened by the NEP and enabled less domestic production.

2. With economic development, the Northern Territories demanded their own royalties and would not relinquish them to Ottawa. The offshore Atlantic provinces certainly argued and obtained these royalties. Ottawa subsidized to the tune of 80% drilling in the Mackenzie Delta Beaufort Sea. Dome Petroleum participated in this with its internally owned drilling contractor CanMar. This was a lucrative government financing of its massive frontier exploration project. The proven natural gas reserves of the Mackenzie Delta were shut in and lost when Justice Berger, Trudeau's appointed saviour, shut down the Mackenzie Delta Pipeline. He actually specified a 10-year delay, which effectively killed the project. Madness! Absolute madness!
3. The theoretical goal of increased Canadian interest in the energy industry was a step backward in that large foreign corporations, especially integrated ones, were better able to deal with massive government interference than smaller entrepreneurial Canadian companies. The big socialist government companies of the time, PetroCanada and Canterra, ultimately returned to private ownership.

CHAPTER 3

Bilingualism

Speaking another language, especially if it's part of one of Canada's founding cultures, is admirable. The problem here was the massive increase of bureaucracy, exorbitant cost and increased one-province bias. The result, although not necessarily the goal, was that this good thought would promote paper at the expense of productivity. The theoretical thought promoted by Trudeau Senior and his separatist Quebec cohort René Lévesque was that this would improve national unity and equality for all Canadians, anglophones and francophones. The power shift's self-focused goal was masked as a noble idea.

First, we saw the institution in the interest of equality of francophone language services across 8 of 10 provinces where there was no demand or need. Jobs and funding exploded and what came out of that? Increased bureaucracy !!! None of it was really productive. We ended up with translators galore all over the place.

Problems were

- unneeded francophone language services in 8 of 10 provinces,
- massive pointless bureaucracy increase,
- Quebec dominance of federal public service, and
- widespread and unnecessary document translation.

The Official Languages Act of 1969 declared the "equality status" of English and French in Parliament, the Canadian Public Service, all federal departments, judicial and quasi-judicial bodies, administrative agencies and crown corporations.[4] Very few at that time recognized the scope of this. The limitations and massive refocus of practical functioning government was mind-boggling.

One of the unproductive parts of this legislation was that all middle management positions in the federal government had to be bilingual. The effective result was that the rule of competency to perform or administer a function within the federal government administration became based more on language than competency. Geographical distribution gave preference to Quebecers whose native tongue was both French and English.

---

[4] "Official Languages Act 1985," Justice Laws Website, https://laws-lois.justice.gc.ca/eng/acts/o-3.01/fulltext.html.

Canada is a large country with great cultural, economic and industrial diversity. There is always a dispute between federal and regional aspects of jurisdiction. When the federal government oversteps its role, the regions are swamped by legislation and administration that are counter to the region's functioning productivity. The United States and Australia have a senate that is elected on a geographical or state-by-state basis, such that the regions cannot be overwhelmed by large urban populations. Canada does not have that protection. This weakens the prosperity of the country as a whole. Regulation of basic socioeconomic parameters from 3,000 kilometres away does not work.

Let us for the moment move forward to the present and observe the statistical situation. Of the significant jobs in the Canadian federal government bureaucratic administration, 43% require French/English bilingualism. The population of Quebec that is bilingual is 58%. Only 12% of Canadians live in Quebec.[5] With the exception of the small, mostly government-dependant province of New Brunswick, only 5–10% of Canadians speak French or are French/English bilingual. The vast majority of the provinces and the people are being ignored. That translates

---

[5] John Ivison, "Concerns Raised as Liberals Consider Tougher French Requirements for Public Servants," October 2017, https://nationalpost.com/opinion/john-ivison-concerns-raised-as-liberals-consider-tougher-linguistic-requirements-for-public-servants.

(pardon my pun) into the vast majority of Canada and Canadians being administered by bureaucrats with a Quebec base. The bureaucracy reigns supreme. They often have no idea of or even concern for what they are doing or regulating. Regulations, bearing in mind the thousands of kilometres of distances and diverse culture, are often vastly inappropriate.

In my brief stint at Northern Affairs in Ottawa, I observed stacks of Northern well schedules translated into French and never used. I am sure this was a minor example of widespread, unused and unnecessary translated documents. The senior engineer was from Egypt and had his position because he spoke French, which was never used. A head of the section was sent on a year's language training and never seen again.

Perhaps one of the more significant tragedies of this remote, insensitive bureaucracy is that local people, whether indigenous or non-indigenous, were and are being denied the wanted benefits of infrastructure projects because decisions are made based on distant dogma rather than local need or values. Many minor projects such as roads, schools or water plants are stalled because of slow or lacking communication from afar.

The cost is enormous and the value negative at best. One wonders how much English/French translation will add to the building and operation of the now government-owned Trans Mountain Pipeline. Productivity and prosperity are again placed in peril by politics.

CHAPTER 4

Better Politics and Movement Forward

Major transgressions of the federal Liberal governments under Senior Prime Minster Trudeau finally had a political fallout. This came partly from its outrageous misjudgements and partly from the accompanying massive corruption.

In 1979, Joe Clark and the Progressive Conservative Party of Canada temporarily ousted the Trudeau government. The Right Honourable Joe Clark, also known as Joe Who, briefly became prime minister. He was, to say the least, ineffectual, and in 1980 the Trudeau Liberal government was returned to power for another four-year term. The Quebec bias, anti-Western Canadian attitude, increased bureaucracy and socialist tendencies continued. Debt financing escalated, and the free enterprise system that built the country continued to be under attack.

In 1984, the Trudeau Senior Liberal government was finally ousted in a more permanent fashion. The Progressive Conservative Party of Canada was elected as a majority government under a new leader. The Honourable Brian Mulroney became Prime Minster of Canada. Hope had risen! He and the Party were less socialist and more free enterprise. He had solid support in Western Canada and Quebec. The Western support came from a better attitude. The Quebec support came from the fact that he was from Quebec. He revoked the dreadful anti-Western Trudeau National Energy Program. He signed the Canada-United States Free Trade Agreement. The relationship between Canada and the United States was better than it had been in decades. Canadian Prime Minister Brian Mulroney and US president Ronald Reagan were Irish buddies. They even shared a friendly baseball rivalry.

During the second term of the Mulroney Government from 1988 to 1993, things again began to fall apart. The Quebec bias, corruption and government overspending resumed. The Central Canada base was again ignoring and taking advantage of Western Canada. In 1991, Lucien Bouchard split out the Bloc Québécois from the Progressive Conservative Party of Canada. This was a pressure for even more power and privilege to Quebec. It destabilized the Party and pushed its focus even further toward central Canada.

In 1987, Preston Manning and others established the Reform Party of Canada to deal with rising sentiments of western discontent and lack of influence in Ottawa. Faith had been lost in the Mulroney Government, which had been propelled into power by the West and was now being ignored. With the rise of the Reform Party and the split out of the Bloc Québécois, the Mulroney government lost the 1993 election.

The Reform Party's chief operating phrase was "the West wants in." A key policy was the Triple-E Senate,[6] which stood for equal, elected and effective. In the United States, each state, regardless of population, has two senators, and they are elected. In the United States, legislation has to be passed by both the House of Representatives, which is population based, and the Senate, which is geographical and region based. This tends to prevent legislation by large, urban populations overriding the interests of the regions with which they may not identify. A similar situation exists in Australia and hence can be compatible with the British Parliamentary system. There is an equal number of senators—12—from each of the six states regardless of population.[7] Their regions are also diverse, with

---

[6] "Reform Party of Canada," https://en.wikipedia.org/wiki/Reform_Party_of_Canada.

[7] "Senate," Parliament of Australia, https://www.aph.gov.au/About_Parliament/Senate.

different socioeconomic bases and cultures. The regions cannot be ignored by a central government in Canberra or high-population areas in Sydney and Melbourne.

This effective regional influence and protection does not exist in Canada. The Senate is appointed and, like the House of Commons, dominated by disproportionally large numbers from the high urban populations of Ontario and Quebec. The result is control and dictatorial authority of the regions—i.e., Western Canada by a central government that is unknowledgeable of and even antagonistic to their socioeconomic, financial and cultural issues.

The other organization coming out of the dissatisfaction of Western Canada with the Central Canada Laurentian elite was the Western Canada Concept (WCC). The WCC was a Western Canadian political party founded in 1980 by Doug Christie and others to promote the separation of the provinces of Manitoba, Saskatchewan, Alberta, British Columbia, the Yukon and the Northwest Territories to form a new nation. It was an entity that could freely develop its own natural resources and that was consistent with their own socioeconomic, financial and cultural values. This would be a self-sufficient, self-determining entity free from hostile regulations four thousand kilometres away with non-representative taxation. Their premise was that the West wanted out of Canada (as opposed to the Reform Party's "the West wants in"). Many think with the current situation the concept is going to be back again with the Wexit Canada Party, advocating for the secession of Western Canada.

The sequence can be summed as

> Liberal > Dissatisfaction > Progressive Conservative > Dissatisfaction > Reform > Alliance > New Conservative.

In the 1993 election, the Reform Party of Canada basically replaced the Progressive Conservatives as the largest political party in Western Canada. The Progressive Conservative Party was reduced to two Members of Parliament. They had sold out Western concerns and suffered politically therefrom. The Reform Party in 1993 elected 52 Members of Parliament from Western Canada and one from Ontario.[8] The Bloc Québécois elected 54 Members of Parliament from Quebec alone. The Bloc, a Quebec separatist entity, took on the role as Leader of the Opposition.[9] Hence we had Jean Chretien of Quebec as the new leader of the Liberal Party as prime minister and Separatist Bloc Québécois Leader Bouchard of the official opposition. The situation was absurd. The West was infuriated, yet with the Quebec bias situation, it was basically impotent and powerless to do anything.

---

[8] Deirdre Mitchell-MacLean, "The Kids in the Reform Party," *Lethbridge Herald*, December 2019, https://lethbridgeherald.com/commentary/opinions/2019/12/10/the-kids-in-the-reform-party/.

[9] "Bloc Québécois Official Opposition," *Canadian Encyclopedia*, 1997, https://thecanadianencyclopedia.ca/en/article/bloc-quebecois.

The Reform Party cause, in addition to the equitable power issue of the Triple-E Senate and associated democratic reform, was the reduction of ever-increasing debt and bloating government bureaucracy. I briefly held a job as a supposed technical bureaucrat in Ottawa with the Federal Department of Northern Affairs. The whole role was unproductive shuffling of paper. One bureaucrat arrived and left on time but spent the bulk of the day in the bar. The Minister of Northern Affairs wanted to have his own group of engineers and geoscientists so that he did not have to consult with those in Energy and Mines. Pointed bureaucratic duplication. Obviously the situation has gotten worse, not better.

With the political splits between the Liberal Party, the separatist Bloc Québécois, the remnant ineffectual Progressive Conservatives and the Reform Party, the government of Canada went through multiple years of unproductive minority governments. The entity coming out on top for the most part was the Quebec-based Liberal Party. This was primarily Prime Minister Jean Chretien and to some extent Paul Martin, the mogul of Canada Steamship Lines, the big importer of Saudi Arabian crude oil. Some progress was made with respect to deficit reduction and non-socialist economic reality, but in general the situation was Eastern biased and functioning poorly. Quebec type corruption and bribery continued to reign supreme. Paper bag cash transfers during the Quebec Referendum and the Sponsorship Scandal were the most blatant.[10]

Eventually, Preston Manning spent brief periods as Leader of the Opposition. Basic issues and discrepancies were obviously not being resolved. In an effort to retrieve from the Liberal left a return to conservative or at least centre-right values, it became obvious that some kind of uniting to end vote splitting was needed. The first attempt at this was in 2000, with the Reform Party revamping its policies and constitution to rebrand as Canadian Alliance. In their Democratic fashion a leadership review was held, and Stockwell Day replaced Preston Manning. Stockwell then became Leader of the Opposition.[11] Concepts fought for by the new Party were financial prudence, elimination of ineffectual social programs and reduced taxation. Nothing was resolved.

For these failed, very temporary months, former Prime Minister Joe Clark was still Red Tory Leader of the remnant Federal Progressive Conservative, and he would not budge.

In December 2005, a vote (plebiscite) was finally allowed by all members of both the Alliance Party and the remnant Federal Progressive Conservative Party. The vote for unification of the two was overwhelming.

---

[10] "Adscam Sponsorship Scandal," https://www.primetimecrime.com/Recent/Investigative/Sponsorship%20Scandal.htm.

[11] Jeffrey Simpson, "The Collapse of Stockwell Day," https://www.theglobeandmail.com/news/politics/the-astonishing-collapse-of-stockwell-day/article760861/.

The new entity would be called the Conservative Party of Canada. Vote splitting and perpetual re-election of Eastern Liberal Socialist governments would come to an end.

In February 2006, the Honourable Stephen Harper was elected prime minister of Canada. He was born in Toronto and attended high school in the suburb of Leaside, Ontario. He was the Member of Parliament for Calgary West and had a degree in economics from the University of Calgary.[12] A voice knowledgeable of Western Canadian values and with training in economics was sure to bring a much-needed revised approach to financial common sense. Things were looking up for the country. It was a time for Western Canada to boom. There was surely to be a better Canada with a hoped-for, more balanced approach in Ottawa.

The price of oil was high, even more than $100 per barrel at times. The price of natural gas, although not high, was stable due to increased demand. Ottawa received billions of dollars of tax revenue from the Western Canadian oil industry. This was deemed fair and balanced. The industry was regulated but was allowed to flourish for the benefit of the west and indeed all of Canada. The somewhat questionable Chretien-introduced policy of equalization[13] was

---

[12] World Health Organization, Prime Minister Stephen Harper, https://www.who.int/topics/millennium_development_goals/accountability_commission/harper/en/.

[13] Edison Roy-Cesar, "Canada's Equalization Formula," https://lop.parl.ca/sites/PublicWebsite/default/en_CA/ResearchPublications/200820E8.

even regarded, with the level of Western prosperity, as being acceptable or at least ignored and tolerated. Equalization was a policy whereby provinces that were doing well financially were obliged to transfer billions of dollars to provinces that were not doing so well. The problem was that these funds went mostly to finance provincial bureaucracy. The other effect was to stall and to instil complacency as to developing their own natural resources. Thus the program perpetuated and tended to make permanent a dependant imbalance. One of the more biased and inequitable aspects of the framework was that the very significant revenues of Hydro Quebec were not included. The Alberta non-renewable resource revenue was.

The times brought new technical innovations that often accompany prosperity and free enterprise opportunities. Two of the most significant for the conventional Western Canadian Energy Industry were fracking and horizontal drilling.

Fracking, or more formally, hydraulic fracturing, is a process of injecting water-based fluids and chemicals into poorly porous hydrocarbon-bearing rock formations. This induces or enhances fractures that allow the flow and production of oil and gas that would otherwise remain trapped in the rock formation.

Horizontal drilling is an astounding process that increases the volume or surface exposure of the potentially productive wellbore to the hydrocarbon-bearing reservoir. Traditional drilling involved the straight downward vertical drilling to the potential hydrocarbon-bearing zone. With horizontal drilling, the well is drilled downward toward the target zone and then curved by sophisticated directional steering techniques to go along the reservoir zone. This could be several hundred metres. Yielded is a producing surface potentially a hundred times greater than that facilitated by the vertical pay zone.

Horizontal drilling was particularly beneficial to the oil industry of Saskatchewan. It involved a well cost three times greater than a conventional vertical well, *but* the production tended to be ten times more. Saskatchewan was transformed from a more minor oil province to production rivalling and on a per capita basis exceeding that of Alberta. The zone of prime interest was the Bakken Formation, which was slightly deeper than the previously established producing zones in Saskatchewan. This zone was the same one that had already fuelled the North Dakota oil boom. Fracking was also involved. Development of this zone would not have been possible without this new technology.

Also helpful to the booming Saskatchewan resource development was Saskatchewan Party Premier Brad Wall. He was a staunch supporter of free enterprise, provincial rights and a fair non-exploitive Canada. He was Premier of Saskatchewan from November 2007 until February 2018. He had replaced a previous, more socialist NDP government. Alberta at this time had been going through some somewhat industry meddlesome Progressive Conservative premiers such as Ed Stelmach and Alison Redford. That probably also helped. With its smaller drilling depths, easier access agricultural road network and lower land costs, Saskatchewan became a popular location for smaller entrepreneurial Canadian companies and start-ups. The less bureaucratic and more responsive government administration and support services also helped. At an oil industry function I attended, Premier Brad Wall jested that being Premier was an easy job, especially in an industry where you just had to try not to do very much. He received loud applause.

Fracking was particularly helpful to the British Columbia oil and natural gas industry. The industry is located in the northeast corner of the province adjacent to Alberta and a long way culturally and geographically from the big urban population centres of Vancouver and Victoria. Due to the rugged terrain, drilling site preparation costs alone can exceed that of simply drilling and completing a well in Saskatchewan. Nonetheless, the fracked and horizontally drilled wells yielded high potential. Tendency was toward natural gas and condensate more than crude oil. Many smaller Canadian companies and start-ups, including Arc, Painted Pony, Peyto, Crew, Tourmaline and Progress were attracted to and made great strides in this higher potential area. Regions like Alberta had seen significant oil and gas development since the early 1950s. The current Fortis Pipeline had been transporting natural gas to the Vancouver area, as well as Pacific Gas and Electric in California since the late 1950s and into the early '60s. Geologically, one of the merits of the area was the multiple number of target formations and potentially productive horizons. The most prolific was the Montney Formation deep below the many established, producing horizons. It was also heavily dependent on the new technologies of fracking and horizontal drilling.

The political component in British Columbia prior to the Horgan NDP was also more or less favourable. The Christy Clark provincial Liberal government realized the financial importance of this economically vibrant although remote component of the provincial economy and tax base. The government support staff and regulator like in Saskatchewan was smaller, less bureaucratic and motivated to be supportive.

In Alberta, the big economic builder of the upbeat Harper years was the oil sands. In had started serious development in the 1960s, but again with the Harper years and new technology, it mushroomed. Major new mining projects were built by multinational and domestic companies. The Canadian majors were Encana, Suncor and Imperial. The newer medium-size Canadian entities were Meg and Canadian Natural. Major improvements were made in settling ponds, pollution control and processing. Much of the new development was coming from in situ steam injection and recovery as opposed to mining. One would have thought environmentalists would have lauded this, but apparently not. Developing and operating these vast industrial complexes in these extremely cold and remote areas is a tribute to Canadian expertise, hard work and ingenuity. It should be praised, not denigrated.

The significant result of all this was a near tripling of crude oil reserves and potential production. The challenge was to get this valuable economic product flowing to market. Major interprovincial and intercontinental pipelines were needed. There were four proposals or potential projects: Northern Gateway, Trans Mountain, Keystone XL and Energy East. The National Energy Board was the competent technical and legal entity for evaluating these projects. It was supposed to evaluate them all. They were a body of highly qualified engineers, scientists, environmentalists, lawyers and negotiators.

The Keystone XL was a pipeline from Alberta to the United States' Gulf Coast, and even with Canadian approval had to be passed by US regulators and politicians. The Energy East project was opposed by and eventually negated by Quebec. The Trans Mountain Project was the simple twinning of an existing pipeline from Alberta to the existing Burnaby oil terminal on the Pacific Coast near Vancouver. The Northern Gateway was a shorter, new oil pipeline from Alberta to the existing deep-water industrial port of Kitimat on the British Columbia North Pacific. It should have been hailed as a major northern development project benefiting indigenous and non-indigenous people in the town of Kitimat and across Northern British Columbia.

The National Energy Board and the Canadian Environmental Assessment Agency spent three and half years thoroughly evaluating the merits and disadvantages of the project. It communicated and consulted with all the indigenous band governments along the route and with the people of Kitimat and other involved Northern BC towns.

In December 2013, the National Board and JRP recommended the project be approved. Sadly, there was a 6-month delay and hesitation by the federal Conservative government, Natural Resources Minister Joe Oliver and then Prime Minister Stephen Harper. Eventually, in June 2014, the then federal government and Prime Minister Stephen Harper proclaimed that the project was in the best interest of Canada and should proceed. Canada was making great strides with its hard work and ingenuity paying off. The project would proceed—albeit with 209 conditions.

CHAPTER 5

Northern Gateway Pipeline

Prior to discussing the Northern Gateway, it is important to discuss the background that facilitated the demand for this massive industrial project. There are numerous conventional oilfields across Northern Alberta that formed an oil exploration and development framework. Perhaps one of the most significant was the Upper Devonian Keg River reef oilfields of Rainbow Lake and Zama Lake in north western Alberta. These were a major area of activity and economic development in the late 1960s.

Nonetheless, it was the Alberta oil sands their gigantic reserves and world-scale production potential that drove the demand for the Northern Gateway Project. Their development represents a monumental achievement. These bitumen-filled sandstone rocks were known to and utilized by the original First Nations Cree inhabitants of the area. They were exposed at the surface, and waters of the Athabasca River had flown over them for thousands of centuries.

The first non-native documentation of the oil sands, tar sands was done by an American fur trader named Peter Pond around 1790. From 1875 to 1882, the Geological Survey of Canada initiated technical evaluation of the tar sands area. Robert Bell of the Survey was the first to suggest the oil development possibilities of the region. It was also noted that water separated the bitumen from the sandstone.

In the 1920s, the newly formed Alberta Research Council developed a hot water extraction process to remove oil trapped in the sand. It even involved a field scale separation plant.[14] The modern-day commercial development of the oil sands began with the construction of the Great Canadian Oil sands plant in 1964. Production began in 1967. Initial production was via a bucket wheel excavator and miles of conveyor belts.[15] The extreme cold temperature and sand wreaked havoc with men and machinery. The temperatures were and still are below -40° C for months on end. Sand ripped conveyor belts and anything mechanical apart. It was a constant struggle to keep vehicles running and

---

[14] "History of the Oil Sands," The Regional Aquatics Monitoring Program (RAMP), http://www.ramp-alberta.org/ramp.aspx.
[15] "Oil Sands Facts and Statistics 2020," Alberta Environment, https://www.alberta.ca/oil-sands-facts-and-statistics.aspx.

personnel from freezing. At the time, this was regarded as a monumental achievement of Canadian ingenuity, technical expertise, hard work and perseverance. It still should be today.

Syncrude began construction of the Mildred Lake facility in 1973 with first production in 1978. This operation, although still mining, used scoop shovels and giant trucks. This proved to be a more positive and less troublesome approach than the Great Canadian oil sands (GCOS) bucketwheel method.

Imperial Oil came into the picture with the first in situ operation. This was at Cold Lake in 1985. Production by 1989 exceeded 140,000 barrels of oil per day. In situ is, unlike the GCOS and Syncrude projects, not a mining operation. Oil is recovered by pumping steam down one wellbore, dissolving the bitumen or heavy oil, and then producing it through the second wellbore. Many of the more recent oil sands projects use this method as opposed to mining. This process is also referred to as SAGD (steam-assisted gravity drainage).[16] Popular environmental protestors and eco-fanatics overuse oil sands mine pictures in an attempt to portray horrific devastation. You would think that they would praise the in situ alternative, but that does not appear to be so.

Many other projects and producers escalated the oil sands to the major economic entity it is today. These

---

[16] "In Situ Bitumen Extraction," *Oil Sands Magazine*, https://www.oilsandsmagazine.com/technical/in-situ.

included newer rapidly growing mid-size Canadian companies such as Canadian Natural Resources and Meg Energy, Canadian majors Petro-Canada, Nexen and Husky, as well as international heavyweights such as Shell, Statoil and Total. Everyone wanted a piece of the pie.

The Alberta or Athabasca oil sands had an astounding 2012 oil production of 1.8 million barrels per day. Of this production, approximately 47% was in situ. The Alberta Energy Regulator reports crude bitumen production of 2.8 million barrels per day for 2017. Sadly, due to pipeline constraints, much of this was being shipped by rail, an uneconomic and relatively less safe alternative. For the fiscal year 2016–17, the Alberta government bitumen royalty totalled $1.48 billion. So much for the far-too-frequent socialist rant about a subsidized fossil fuel industry.

The oil sands bitumen in place can be estimated at between 1.3 and 1.7 trillion barrels of oil. The International Energy Agency (IEA) has estimated recoverable reserves at 178 million barrels of oil. This equates to Canada having, after Saudi Arabia and Venezuela, the third-largest recoverable crude oil reserves in the world. Of this, it is expected that 80% [17] would be recoverable by in situ or SAGD instead of mining.

The Fort McMurray or Athabasca oil sands have

---

[17] Oil Sands Economic Contributions Natural Resources Canada https://www.nrcan.gc.ca/energy/publications/18756

been subjected to worldwide abuse and denigration by emotion-based, supposed environmental organizations. Much of this is unwarranted. Major improvements in settling ponds and reduced emissions go unnoticed[18]. These involve groundwater monitoring, flocculants for settling as well as soil and boreal forest vegetation replacement. These were particular efforts of the Industry. The fact that in situ production and not mining will be the major (80%) ongoing production method is again unacknowledged.

Perhaps another worldwide misrepresentation is that this project negatively affects First Nations. The Fort Mackay Nation led by Chief Boucher is a multimillion-dollar contractor to the oil sands industry.[19] The wealth has given unheard of funding for the development of schools and infrastructure not only for their band but across the province. Their unemployment rate is so low that they bring in and train other indigenous people from as far away as the Blood Reservation in southern Alberta. The oil and gas industry is the largest employer of First Nations people in Canada. The median employment income for Fort McKay First Nations ($61,248) exceeds that for every province except Alberta ($64,090). Fort McMurray First Nations show a median income ($52,480) above those of five provinces

---

[18] Oil Sands: Tailings Management Natural Resources Canada https://www.nrcan.gc.ca/energy/publications/18752

[19] Gordon Kent, "Fort McKay Chief Jim Boucher Named Energy Person of the Year," https://edmontonjournal.com/business/energy/fort-mckay-chief-jim-boucher-named-canadian-energy-person-of-the-year.

(Manitoba, Nova Scotia, Quebec, New Brunswick and Prince Edward Island).

Upside production for the Athabasca oil sands had been predicted to be some five million barrels per day by 2028. With project cancellations and a slower rate of growth, the Canadian Association of Petroleum Producers had predicted for 2020 a per-day production of 3.3 million.

This was and is the massive background of hard work, capital investment and productivity that built up to the need for the Northern Gateway proposal. Before we proceed to the actual pipeline discussion, let us put some dollar figures on the assets involved. Let us use $15 per barrel, $30 per barrel and 300 days per year. The $15 could represent the restricted pipeline access and rail transport value. The $30 is a theoretical price for adequate pipeline access and minimal rail transport.

For 2017, the annual production from 2.8 million per day would calculate to 840 million barrels. At $15 per barrel, that would be $12.8 billion, and at $30 per barrel, it would be $25.2 billion. For 2020, with a possible or projected 3.3 million per day, this would be an annual production of 990 million barrels. At $15 per barrel, that would be $14.85 billion, and at $30 it would be $29.7 billion. For 2028 and a projected five million barrels per day, the annual production would be 1500 million barrels. At $15 per barrel, that is $22.5 billion, and $30 it is a mindboggling $45 billion.

Using these figures, one can calculate for 2020 a

pipeline versus no pipeline difference of $14.85 billion, and for 2028 a whopping $22.5 billion. These are the massive asset values at stake.

The concept of a Northern Gateway Pipeline to link the Alberta oil sands with the British Columbia coast was first suggested by Enbridge Inc. in 2002. They subsequently paused while considering alternate routes through the United States. Encouragement from producers subsequently reinforced the Northern Gateway route.

Enbridge announced officially in 2008 its intention to build the Northern Gateway pipeline. This would be a route to get the massive multibillion-dollar Alberta oil sands asset to tidewater and lucrative overseas markets. The 1,177-kilometre pipeline would run from Bruderheim, Alberta, to Kitimat, British Columbia. Kitimat had already been established as an industrial city with the building of the Aluminium Company (AlCan) of Canada smelter some 60 years ago. It had a deep-water, ocean-access port at Douglas Channel.

In December 2009, the National Energy Board and the Canadian Environmental Assessment Agency issued the terms of reference for the environmental and regulatory review of the Northern Gateway Pipeline. They would function together as the JRP. This was its first public announcement. The government requirements that the proponent is to follow concerning resource development, regulation, economics, indigenous consultation and the environment were laid out in a step-by-step detailed plan by qualified experts and professionals.

In May 2010, Enbridge submitted its project application to the Joint Review Panel. It consisted of eight volumes of detailed information based on the published requirements. In July 2010, the Joint Review Panel issued a procedural directive requesting comments on the issues listed and additional information that Enbridge should be required to file, as well as oral hearing locations.

In August 2010, the Canadian Environmental Assessment Agency and the National Energy Board (JRP) held a public session. The purpose of the session was to allow public discussion on issues and information relative to the Enbridge Pipeline application. The circus began.

In January 2011, the Joint Review Panel requested that Enbridge provide additional information on the design and risk assessment of the pipeline due to the difficult access and unique geographic location of the project. The oil and gas industry had been drilling, completing wells and building local pipelines in these areas for decades. The challenges of operating major projects in the sometimes-hostile environment of Northern Alberta and Northeast British Columbia had been met by the industry and successfully dealt with. The panel was perhaps the one without the experience. Nonetheless, Enbridge complied with the request.

The Enbridge proposal consisted of two pipelines:

one to transport heavy crude from the oil sands at Ft. MacMurray in Alberta to a coastal terminal at Kitimat British Columbia, the second an auxiliary line to transport imported condensate and lighter liquids from the coastal port to the pipeline source.

The Joint Review Panel, consisting of the National Energy Board and the Canadian Environmental Assessment Agency, officially began hearings in January 2012 with a planned completion date and a report with recommendations to be completed in early 2013. The combined technical expertise of engineers, biologists, geo-technicians, hydrogeologists, archaeologists, accountants, lawyers and miscellaneous experts had to be formidable.

In March 2013, the Federal Natural Resources Minister announced changes or improvements to marine safety rules for oil tankers.

In April 2013, the JRP issued an additional list of the 199 conditions Enbridge would have to meet upon pipeline approval.

In May 2013, the BC government informed the JRP that they do not support the pipeline.

In August 2013, Natural Resources Minister Joe Oliver required companies to have a billion-dollar bond to cover the remote possibility of an oil spill.

In November 2013, British Columbia Premier Christy Clark and Alberta Premier Alison Redford reached an agreement to support the pipeline.

In November 2013, unfounded popular protests

occurred in Vancouver and across Canada against the pipeline. Protests were mostly led by paid organizers. Most participants were motivated by general vague "green" ideologies. They, in general, knew not where, why or what about the actual pipeline, but they were loud and motivated about that which would affect them in no way whatsoever. Strange!

Decisions with regard to major economic projects in a sane society need to be made by technically qualified and financially responsible individuals. The engineers, biologists, geo-technicians, hydrogeologists, archaeologists, lawyers and miscellaneous experts of the JRP were such individuals. The review process was both comprehensive and locally focused. The review involved some 180 hearing days, 175,000 pages of evidence, 9,400 letters, 1,179 oral presentations, 389 witnesses and 60 interviews.

With this solid community and technical support, the Joint Review Panel in December 2013 rightly recommended the approval of the Northern Gateway Project. This was followed by a six-month delay and hesitation by the federal Conservative government, Resources Minister Joe Oliver and then Prime Minister Stephen Harper. Eventually, in June 2014, the federal government and the prime minister proclaimed that the project was in the best interest of Canada and should proceed. This was done in the interest of responsible and much-needed sustainable Northern Development.[20] The project had the significant approval of the vast majority of the bands along the actual pipeline route. The indigenous people and bands along the route had signed on and were looking forward to the jobs, opportunity and prosperity that the project would bring, Economic opportunity at home without having to escape to the city for employment or remain on the reservation and government welfare.

In October 2015, a new Liberal government was elected in Ottawa. They were going to protect indigenous people and Western Canadians from themselves. Prime Minster Justin Trudeau, from the other side of the country, put forward a universal ban on oil tanker traffic on the North Coast of British Columbia.

This was a biased decision that did not apply to marine traffic on the East Coast, the St. Lawrence or southern British Columbia. This effectively killed the project. In 2016, Justin Trudeau officially overruled the previous green light and cancelled approval of the project. It appeared that if former Prime Minister Stephen Harper approved of something, Justin Trudeau was against it. One can't help but think if the previous Conservative government had gone with the JRP recommendation more directly, the project would have been underway

---

[20] "Northern Gateway Pipeline Project," Natural Resources Canada, https://www.nrcan.gc.ca/our-natural-resources/energy-sources-distribution/clean-fossil-fuels/pipelines/energy-pipeline-projects/northern-gateway-pipelines-project/19184.

and more difficult to cancel. Nonetheless, it was water under the bridge. The intensive technical review and massive community support mattered not to Trudeau's personal political expediency.

In June 2019, the Trudeau tanker ban bill was passed by the Liberal majority Parliament and the Liberal -dominated Senate, bringing into force bill C-48, the Oil Tanker Moratorium Act. This prohibited oil tanker traffic from the Alaskan border to the northern tip of Vancouver Island. An exception was local transport under 12,500 tons. This effectively put the final nail in the Northern Gateway Project coffin.

Let us summarize what has gone on here.

- In 2008, Enbridge announces its intention to build Northern Gateway.
- In 2009, the National Energy Board and Environmental Assessment Agency issue the terms of reference for the review.
- As the JRP, they lay out a step-by-step plan.
- Regulations and indigenous consultation are to be done by qualified experts.
- In May 2010, Enbridge submits its application to the JRP. It consists of eight volumes of information, as per the published guidelines.
- July 2010, JRP asks for input on issue list, extra info and oral hearing places.
- In August 2010, JRP holds public information session.

- In January 2011, JRP requests additional information on design and risks.
- In January 2012, JRP begins hearings
- In March 2013, Premier Christy Clark announces BC approval of the project.
- In December 2013, with community and technical support, JRP recommends approving the project.
- Six months later, Prime Minster Harper approves the project.
- In January 2016, Prime Minster Justin Trudeau cancels project approval.

Canada forward and backward, after years of work, many more of debate and hundreds of millions of investments, it went absolutely nowhere. Review cost $100 million more or less. Potential annual revenue loss was $15–$22 billion. Prosperity thwarted by politics toward peril and poverty.

CHAPTER 6

Miscellaneous Issues and Events

Let's look at some other events and causes in the once-great nation of Canada heading from prosperity into peril. We shall discuss the Pacific Northwest LNG Project, Energy East, Nunavut, Huawei and Equalization. Nunavut was a government power struggle with considerable waste. Huawei was sheer stupidity. Equalization is another power grab disguised as a noble idea.

The Pacific Northwest LNG Project was first proposed in 2013. The project was led by the Malaysian petroleum-giant Petronas and also involved smaller Canadian producers such as Painted Pony and Progress. The $36 billion project would have seen a natural gas liquefaction and export terminal constructed on British Columbia's northern coast, as well as a new pipeline. The terminal would have been built on Lelu Island, which sits at the mouth of the Skeena River near Prince Rupert, British Columbia. Communities in Prince Rupert and along the pipeline route supported the project for the socioeconomic benefits it would bring. In order to consolidate the supply of natural gas potential production and reserves Petronas took over Progress. After three years of study and consultation, the project was approved by the federal government in September 2016.[21]

The socialist NDP/Green government of John Horgan and Andrew Weaver was elected and manoeuvred into power in May 2017. With the antidevelopment stance of the NDP/Green government, Petronas withdrew from the project in July 2017. These gigantic northeast British Columbia proven and productive natural gas reserves will, with the Shell LNG Canada Project, again obtain a potential overseas market. The three-year delay and proponent switch was still a peril for prosperity. Small Canadian entrepreneurial companies such as Painted Pony and others dropped their share price and equity value from $10 per share to 60 cents. The Shell project, although an ultimate admirable solution,

---

[21] Claudia Capilaneo and G. Morgan, "Pacific Northwest LNG, 2012–17: How to Kill an LNG project in Canada," *Financial Post*, July 2017, https://business.financialpost.com/commodities/energy/pacific-northwest-lng-2012-2017-how-to-kill-an-lng-project-in-canada.

involved multiyear delays, increased costs and decreased Canadian participation. The great Canadian Socialist government of Horgan Weaver did the same "delay and increased cost" thing with the Site C dam project, which they also campaigned against and then ran with out of economic necessity.

Nunavut is the largest and most northerly territory in Canada. It includes most of the Arctic Archipelago and some of the northeast portion of the former NWT mainland. It has a population of 38,780 (Stats Can 2019).

The Arctic Islands are a truly wondrous place. They have magnificent glaciers that stream out of the mountains into an azure ocean, with picturesque patches of white snow. The muskeg pastures flourish in the summer and support significant herds of hairy muskox and numerous arctic hare. How they survive through the brutal winters is beyond comprehension. The glorious mountain ranges of Ellesmere and Axel Heiberg Island block the polar winds and with the warm Gulf Stream currents provide quite reasonable summer temperatures.

The geology of the Arctic Islands is magnificent and, with minimal vegetation, exposed in its grandeur for all to see. The geology indicated vast oil and gas resource potential. Initial exploration and development came out of Western Canada via Edmonton and Yellowknife. The original Canadian push into this territory came from the Department of Transport weather stations.

The operation centre was Resolute Bay, with outpost stations at Eureka on Ellesmere and Isaksen on Ellef Ringnes. This weather station government operation was a license to print money for the Power Corporation du Canada out of Montreal that had the government contract to run it.

The problem came with the resource development leading the natural practical route out of Edmonton and Yellowknife. Quebec was deeply threatened by the potential loss of domain. Nunavut was designated into a separate political division and territory in 1999 via the Nunavut Act. Why have we created a separate political entity for 40,000 people?[22] Quebec and government bureaucracy, that's why. Divert the flow out of Yellowknife and back to Frobisher Bay, Iqaluit and Montreal. A whole sitting legislature for 40,000 people in the middle of nowhere. Once again, we have prosperity in peril.

Energy East was a proposed oil pipeline that would transport oil sands crude oil and other production to existing Canadian refineries in New Brunswick and Quebec. It would, among other things, facilitate having more Canadian oil refined in Canada. This concept of refining Canadian crude oil production in Canada was an answer to the oft-voiced concern of the socialist left that we should process rather than export raw products. The $12 billion project was first announced

---

[22] Kenneth John Rea, "Nunavut Territory Canada," https://www.britannica.com/place/Nunavut.

in August 2013. It would have been a great Canadian achievement, the longest pipeline in North America.

Let us take a look at the process for putting this great-for-Canada project together. Evaluation and hearings were to be conducted by the National Energy Board (NEB).

April 2014: funding was available to participate in the NEB hearing process; in October, NEB received Trans Canada's application.

February 2015: Federal Court denied Interlocutory injunction motion; in March, NEB to allow people more time to participate; in July, NEB issued list of Aboriginal intervenors; in October, NEB to hear oral Aboriginal traditional evidence.

March 2016: NEB reopened public process to participate; in April, NEB released preliminary timeline; in June, NEB doubled participant funding to $10 million; in August, hearing scheduled to start in New Brunswick, with public proceedings in Quebec; August Montreal session postponed; August suspension of panel sessions; in September, panel steps down.

No wonder the process got clogged up when you put up $10 million to join. Aboriginals couldn't even make an effort to write their report.

In January 2017, the Energy East hearings were to restart from the beginning.[23]

---

[23] [21] Warren Mabee, "What Really Sank the Energy East Pipeline," https://www.nationalobserver.com/2017/10/20/analysis/what-really-sank-energy-east-pipeline.

On Wednesday August 28, 2017, the NEB was replaced by the Canadian Energy Regulator (CER). In October 2017, Trans Canada withdrew its Energy East and eastern mainline project applications. With the switch to the CER also came revised terms of reference. Downstream as well as retail gasoline emissions were to be added as remote factors in project evaluation. Also, the step-by-step logical evaluation process as discussed previously was being overridden with political bureaucrats replacing technical and professional evaluators. Trans Canada, like Kinder Morgan, had to call an end to the perpetual dealing with bureaucratic, judicial and political hoops going nowhere. Denis Coderre, the mayor of Montreal, celebrated. Again the Quebec politicos won and Canada lost.

There are other variations on the Energy East theme. Oceangoing tankers could upload Western Canadian crude oil at the Port of Montreal. If foreign crude oil can be onloaded, then domestic crude can be uploaded. If oil tankers can come down the St. Lawrence River, they can also travel up. Connecting oil pipelines, such as Enbridge's Line 9, may have to be expanded or twinned to get the western crude to Montreal. Smaller tankers could transit the Great Lakes locks, and marine transport could occur today from Duluth, Minnesota, the termination point of Enbridge's Line 3. The reversal of the old, currently out of use Portland, Maine, to Montreal pipeline also has possibilities. There is currently a proposal before the state of Maine to allow the old offload port facilities to be converted into an upload export mode.[24] This could in theory be an export port for Canadian oil.

Meng Wanzhou, the CFO of the large Chinese computer company **Huawei,** was arrested at the Vancouver airport in December 2018. The United States had charged Meng and Huawei with bank and wire fraud in violation of the American sanctions on Iran. In March 2019, Canada agreed with the US's extradition request.

Finally, after 13 months, her trial began in January 2020. The trial could last months or even years. Two Canadians have been jailed in China and unfairly charged with espionage with what appears to be an unsubstantiated vendetta.[25] Billions of dollars' worth of agricultural exports consisting of pork and soybeans have been blocked. Western Canadian farmers in particular have been economically devastated. If Wenzhou arrived here, and there was a warrant for her arrest, why wasn't she rejected at immigration and put back on a plane to the United States? If there was no warrant present, why wasn't she allowed to proceed to China? This was an American Chinese issue, so why

---

[24] Charles Shaver, "Alberta, Quebec Both Stand to Benefit from Sending Oil Eastward," *The Chronical Herald*, April 2019, https://www.thechronicleherald.ca/opinion/charles-shaver-alberta-quebec-both-stand-to-benefit-from-sending-oil-eastward.

[25] Arjun Kharpal, "The Extradition Trial of Huawei's CFO Starts This Month—Here's What to Watch," CNBC, January 2020.

were Canadian citizens in China and western Canadian farmers made to suffer for it?

Equalization is a federal government program designed, in theory, to share wealth between Canada's have and have-not provinces. It is a gift to provincial governments, not the people of a have-not province. The program was instituted in 1957 but became more onerous with changes in 2004, 2007 and 2009. The program addresses the ability of a provincial government to raise tax revenue from five categories: personal income taxes, business income taxes, consumption (sales) taxes, property taxes and natural resource revenue. That is referred to as fiscal capacity. To determine eligibility, each province's per capita fiscal capacity is compared to average per capita fiscal capacity of the 10 provinces.[26] For the years 2013–14, equalization payments totalled an alarming $16.1 billion. Quebec, the largest recipient, received 48.6% or $7.8 billion. Prince Edward Island on a per capita basis received $2,326. In the pre-2004 formula, Alberta's resource revenues were included in the equalization calculations but were kept out of the standard by which entitlement was determined. Since

---

[26] Edison Roy-Cesar, "Canada's Equalization Formula," Economics, Resources and International Affairs Division Publication No. 2008-20-E, Sept 2013, https://lop.parl.ca/sites/PublicWebsite/default/en_CA/ResearchPublications/.

2007, Alberta's energy resources have been included in the standard.[27]

The level of these payments is outrageous. They go to fatten bureaucracy in provincial governments. They take from the residents of the *have* provinces but do not help the residents of the *have-not* provinces. One of the great inequities is that the very significant revenues of Hydro Quebec are not included when their equalization gift is calculated. It would probably erase the allocation. Alberta, with the four-year federal government's strangulation on pipelines, is currently running a deficit while Quebec, with its equalization benefits, is running a budget surplus.

Another negative of the program is that it entrenches apathy and lack of motivation to proceed toward increased economic activity. The classic curse of government welfare. Five to six years ago, New Brunswick had a small but growing onshore natural gas industry. Among the participants were a small Halifax-based energy company called Corridor Resources. They were drilling, fracking and developing the producing McCully Field. In 2014, the province elected Brian Gallant and the Provincial Liberal Party. They banned fracking and shut down development in the Field and regionally in the Elgin Basin. How noble, you say.

---

[27] Kevin Carmichael, "Getting the Facts Straight When It Comes to Equalization Payments," *Financial Post*, August 2019, https://business.financialpost.com/news/economy/getting-the-facts-straight-when-it-comes-to-provincial-equalization-payments.

But they continued to accept equalization payments partially funded by Alberta and BC fracked natural gas. During the same period, they imported fracked natural gas from New England. Not noble but hypocritical! For years the same company has been trying to develop hydrocarbon potential onshore and offshore Anticosti Island.

The Quebec government stalls and regulates barriers. The large, geophysical Old Harry Prospect has sat undrilled for years. Hydro Quebec's revenue for 2018 was $14.3 billion, and the company is 100% owned by the province of Quebec. Quebec's receipt for equalization for the 2019–20 financial year will be $13.3 billion.[28] I guess the unfairly not included revenue takes care of that. The percentage of government employment in the Maritimes and Quebec is as a result disproportionately and unhealthily high. In PEI, it approaches a unproductive 50%.

Another problem with equalling out dollars is that costs are not added to the equation. The same applies to income tax rates. In New Brunswick, a single-family bungalow may cost $165,000; that same house in Montreal costs $320,000; that same house in

---

[28] Steve Faguy, "Quebec 2019–20 Budget Highlights," *Montreal Gazette*, March 2019, https://montrealgazette.com/news/quebec/quebec-2019-20-budget-highlights.

Toronto costs $950,000; it costs $420,000 in Calgary and $1,200,000 in Vancouver. Again the program has done more to un-equalize than to equalize. More wheel spinning.

CHAPTER 7

Climate Change

In December 2015, Canada sent a delegation of some 300-plus politicians, youth, staff and bureaucrats to the Paris Accord Climate Conference. Perhaps for most this was a paid four-day vacation. Most had few or no technical qualifications. This delegation was double the size of an equivalent US delegation, a country with a population ten times that of Canada. The United Kingdom delegation was 100. The figures from CTV suggest $650,000 for the federal portion alone of the delegation.

This new Paris Agreement is proposed to strengthen the effort to limit the global average temperature rise to 1.5 to 2.0° C. The Paris Agreement undertook to recognize the essential roles of national and subnational governments, cities, the private sector and financial institutions to respond to climate change. The agreement also stated the need to respect, promote and consider the rights of indigenous peoples, local communities and human rights in general when tackling climate change issues.[29] In November 2016, Canada submitted its long-term low greenhouse gas development strategy to the UNFCCC (United Nations Framework Convention on Climate Change). The mid-century climate change strategy looked beyond 2030 to a more sustainable 2050. It seems governments, circumstances and policies change every five years. Forecasters have trouble predicting snow, sunshine or rain next week.

The Paris Agreement stated that developed countries continue to have an obligation to provide financial resources to assist developing countries combat the possible problems of climate change. Parties are invited to prepare and communicate adaptation plans and priorities. Also stated is a need to address loss and damage associated with climate change. No statement is made as to how to verify, evaluate or support said damage, loss or claim. Canada ratified the Paris Agreement with a vote in Parliament in October 2016. Sadly, even the wishy-washy Conservative Opposition Leader intimidated his MPs into supporting the Paris Agreement. With all his carbon tax condemnation, what a hypocrite!

---

[29] Government of Canada, "The Paris Agreement," https://www.canada.ca/en/environment-climate-change/services/climate-change/paris-agreement.html.

Upon the signing of this agreement at the United Nations in New York, Prime Minister Justin Trudeau stated that Canada's efforts to combat climate change will not cease. He praised the business case for clean energy, maintaining that $300 billion had been invested globally therein. A surprising remark from someone who has no sense of business or investment. He went on to say that developing countries should not be punished for a problem caused by developed countries. He then stated that his government was committed to spending $2.65 billion to help developing countries fight climate change. In June 2017, Trudeau launched the $2 billion Low Carbon Economy Fund.[30] The theory said it was designed to support projects that would generate clean growth and reduce greenhouse gas emissions. The reality was that it would throw out grant money and encourage industry to sign on to Trudeau's climate agenda.

He was then thanked and praised for his commitment and funding promise by UN Secretary Ban Ki-moon. The promotion and propaganda purported that climate action is essential to achieve sustainable development goals. The reason 100-plus smaller, less-than-democratic developing countries are signatories and on their side is *the money.*

---

[30] "Businesses and Environmental Groups Urge Canadian Prime Minister and Premiers to Put Low Carbon Economy on the Agenda of Montreal Meeting," *National Observer*, December 2018, https://www.nationalobserver.com/2018/12/06/news/businesses-and-environmental-groups-urge-canadian-prime-minister-and-premiers-put.

To finance and implement this wondrous and "noble" cause, the Liberal government of Canada had the wonderful concept of a "carbon" tax. It is actually a tax on carbon dioxide, but carbon sounds so much more onerous and evil. Dan McTeague of Canadians for Affordable Energy predicted that this would result in drivers paying an additional seven to eight cents per litre on gasoline. With the carbon tax on natural gas, the added cost of heating your home is estimated to be $300 to $400 per year. Much of Canada's food supply is transported from Mexico, California or Florida. Growing of fresh fruits and vegetables is not remotely possible in the six months of Canadian Winter. The tax is on non-optional transported produce. Basic foodstuffs are neither a choice or luxury. This tax will significantly add to the monthly family grocery bill for rich and poor alike.

Repeat after me: "Canada is uninhabitable without fossil fuels." In January 2020, Alberta experienced a brutal cold snap in Red Deer and across southern Alberta to lows of -34 °C. David Yager, in his recent book *From Miracle to Menace: Alberta, A Carbon Story*, states the current debate about climate change and what humankind should do about it has deteriorated to the to the point of absurdity.[31] Climate change in Canada

---

[31] [29] "Repeat after Me, 'Canada Is Uninhabitable Without Fossil Fuels,'" *Alberta Press Reader*, January 2020, https://albertapressleader.ca/repeat-after-me-canada-is-uninhabitable-without-fossil-fuels/.

is a weapon, not an environmental concern. Its goal is to shift power to a socialist central government.

Trudeau's carbon (carbon dioxide) tax grab was announced for 2022 to be $8.2 billion.[32] Much of this money will go to African and Islamic dictatorships. It is said that Canada produces some 1.6% of world carbon emissions, contrasted with China producing 26%. Ironically, Canada contributes millions of dollars to rich, affluent China in the name of this cause.

The tax has been imposed by the federal government against the wishes of at least four provinces: Alberta, Ontario, New Brunswick and Manitoba. The rationale of the Trudeau government is that increased prices will cause consumers to reduce their consumption and hence reduce these planet-threatening fuel and heating sources. Canada is a large and cold country with imported food sources. Heating your home in the winter is not a choice. Getting to work by car, bus or train is not a choice. Transporting goods and people between cities across large geographical distances is not a choice. Consuming imported foodstuffs in the winter is not a choice.

The carbon dioxide tax, deceptively referred to as the carbon tax, was not a mechanism to reduce greenhouse gas emissions. It was and is an out and out tax grab. Increased taxes do nothing for climate change or the

---

[32] Kenneth Green and Ross McKittrick, "A Tax Grab Cloaked in Green," Fraser Institute, https://www.fraserinstitute.org/article/tax-grab-cloaked-green.

environment; they punish already overtaxed Canadians and facilitate increased government bureaucracy. Again we see the Trudeau government masking its devious goals of increased taxation to fund it's bureaucracy with virtue signalling rhetoric.

In 2018, Parliament passed the Greenhouse Gas Pollution Pricing Act. Increased pricing by increased taxation does not deter purchase of the necessities of life. This is an example of the great Canadian flaw of much ado about nothing and the march from prosperity to peril.

The major environmental culprits in the world are by far China and India, and they go ignored. Is that because it would be illegal to protest there? If you protest in China, you go to jail or simply disappear. Perhaps it is that the background goal of world socialism has already been obtained there.

The great climate change hysteria is a *weapon* used by world socialists to shut down free enterprise economic development across the globe. Distinguished MIT atmospheric physicist Richard Lindzen concluded that global warming is about power and politics rather than science.[33] It is a weapon used by Prime Minister Trudeau to cripple and shut down the Canadian oil and gas industry and free enterprise Western Canada in general. He is 100% the Quebec Prime Minster.

---

[33] Richard Lindzen, "Global Warming, Models and Language" in *Climate Change: The Facts*, ed. Alan Moran (Melbourne Australia Institute of Public Affairs, 2015).

Quebec could but does not have an oil and gas industry. Its economic industries are cement, forestry, mining, pharmaceuticals and manufacturing. Its economic wealth is hydroelectricity generated by massive networks of northern dammed rivers. Hydro Quebec is a government entity and can be classified as Green. Many of Quebec's manufacturers, such as Bombardier, are government subsidized to the point of almost being a government entity. This is the background that readily facilitates Mr. Trudeau's socialist anti-oil and gas stance. When one looks at the world, some of the great proponents of the climate change and anti-fossil fuel movement are Germany, Italy and France. Those countries do not have those resources. Russia, Australia and the Middle East are developing their oil and gas resources and prosperity without getting bogged down with the climate hysteria.

Quebec does need oil gas for heating and transportation, just like the rest of Canada. Currently, it begrudgingly gets a little less than half its supply from Western Canada. Its major supplier and favourite trading partner is the Middle East. Since Trudeau's election, the supply of crude oil into Quebec and Eastern Canada has increased by more than 60%. So much for the Green agenda. Up rears the ugly head of engineering company SNC-Lavalin, Mr. Trudeau's king of bribery and corruption. They and their Quebec Caisse Populaire major shareholder have major contracts in the

Saudi Arabian oil and gas industry. If Mr. Trudeau has any affinity to oil and gas, it is there.

The climate change weapon has a widespread, powerful and well-paid support lobby. Vocal environmental voices such as the Tides Foundation and Greenpeace have foreign nation funding. Their energy industry is protected from Canadian competition.

Researcher Vivian Krause has led a concerted effort to expose and fight against the effort by US oil interests to landlock Canadian oil and gas. They have been funding and supporting supposed environmental groups to protest against the industry with the aim of stalling and stopping development. Her background was defending the farmed salmon industry. She noted, while examining the tax forms of the Rockefeller Brothers Fund, the phrase "tar sands campaign," and that in 2007 the fund had donated $1.4 million to an entity called Corporate Ethics. Their campaign goal was "to recruit groups, develop strategy and create a campaign." Executive director Michael Marx boasted that the strategy was to landlock tar sands crude such that it could not get to international markets. So much for the self-motivated will of Canadian protesters. Yes, that is the Rockefeller Family of Standard Oil, ExxonMobil and the Seven Sisters. The CEO of Corporate Ethics boasted of their success at blocking pipelines such as Northern Gateway.³⁴ The resulting price gap between US and Alberta oil sands crude was a financial gain for US refiners and a billion dollar loss to the Canadian industry and Canadians at large. The CEO also bragged of skewing Canadian election results toward the anti-industry Trudeau Liberals as opposed to the more industry-supportive Conservatives. Blatant corruption of our democracy, but it helped Trudeau and the Laurentian elite. So no quarrel.

The weapon and the campaign continues and even escalates. In September 2019, activist Tzeporah Berman, the anti-Alberta colleague of NDP Premier Racheal Notley, received $2 million from an American entity to engineer a large reduction in new oil and gas development that would ensure that huge amounts of carbon stay out of the atmosphere. The request is to shun Canadian products until the "planet-killing tar sands are shut down."³⁵

We are seeing a movement so bent on achieving its political objectives that it is willing to corrupt the science on which they are supposedly based. The issue and the appeal is emotional and far removed from factual

---

[34] Licia Corbella, "Researcher Exposes Money Trail Behind US-Based Campaign to Kill the Oil Sands," *Calgary Herald*, January 2019, https://calgaryherald.com/news/local-news/corbella-vivian-krause-should-become-a-household-name-across-canada.

[35] Stewart Muir, "$2 Million US Gift Proves Again That "Dark Money" Is Mostly on the Anti Oil and Gas Development," *Energy Now*, September 2019, https://energynow.ca/2019/09/2-million-u-s-gift-proves-again-that-dark-money-is-mostly-on-the-anti-oil-and-gas-development-side-stewart-muir/.

science. The repeated use of the term "climate denier" is somewhere between emotional and fearmongering.[36] It is hateful and demeaning to Holocaust survivors. We are seeing governments proceed in the name of this corrupt science to use or attempt to use their regulatory power to implement a massive program of social engineering on the pretext of saving the planet. The root source of this is a United Nations corrupted by the third world. In pompous self-interest, they are requesting that the world must change their eating, transportation, heating, industry, prosperity, happiness and welfare for the shaky, unsubstantiated concept of climate change.[37] George Orwell, in his book *1984*, thought we would be frightened by "Big Brother." Apparently not.

Ninety-seven percent of scientists agree, with regard to man-made global warming, that the idea is parroted over and over again by people in positions of power and influence with no scientific background. It a misconception propagated by two University of Illinois researchers Doran and Zimmerman. In 2009, they sent a survey to 10,257 earth scientists. Many of the respondents indicated that they believed that natural forces were more important than humankind's paltry contributions to climate trends. Some questioned the

---

[36] Patrick Moore, Interview with Danielle Smith, *Global News CHQR*, January 2020.

[37] Michael Hart, *Hubris: The Troubling Science, Economics and Politics of Climate Change* (Ottowa: Compleat Desktops Publishing, 2015).

validity of models that attributed the climate change to carbon dioxide. It wasn't the kind of response that the researchers were looking for. So they arbitrarily decided that 10,180 of the scientists (those not fitting the researchers' goal) weren't qualified to comment on the topic. They were merely solar scientists, space scientists, cosmologists, physicists, meteorologists or astronomers. The field was then limited to 77. Of these, 75 agreed that humankind was causing catastrophic changes to climate.[38] Hence came the 97% consensus to their predetermined premise that humankind was at fault.

Another phrase repeatedly used by the left-wing perpetuators of the climate cause is "science says," and if you don't believe in science, you are too ignorant to be listened to, so there.

Dr. Judith Curry is a PhD climatologist and former chair of the School of Earth and Atmospheric Sciences at the Georgia Institute of Technology. She discusses in her blog *Climate, Etc.*, "Why I Don't Believe in Science."

"I believe in science" is an homage given to science by people who generally don't understand much about it. Science is used here not to describe specific methods or theories but to provide a badge of tribal identity, which serves, ironically, to demonstrate a lack of interest in the guiding principles of actual science.

Elizabeth Warren stated recently in pretty typical

---

[38] Rich Trzupeck, "Krugman Fails Science 101," *Front Page* magazine, August 2011.

form: "I believe in science. And anyone who doesn't has no business making decisions about our environment." This was in response to news that scientists who are skeptical of global warming might be allowed to have a voice in shaping public policy.

"I believe in science" is almost always invoked these days in support of one particular scientific claim: catastrophic anthropogenic global warming. It is in support of one particular political solution: massive government regulations to limit or ban fossil fuels. The problem is the word "belief." Science isn't about belief. It's about facts, evidence, theories and experiments. You don't say, "I believe in thermodynamics." You understand its laws and the evidence for them, or you don't. Belief doesn't really enter into it. There are a lot of people these days who like things that sound science-y but have little patience for actual science.[39] Far too many of Canada's political leaders, media, bureaucrats and supposed educators fit into the Elizabeth Warren category. Prime Minister Justin Trudeau and Catherine McKenna, the former Minister of the Environment, would be among the more prominent culprits.

The corrupted pseudoscience weapon of climate hysteria arbitrarily dismisses hundreds of critical colleagues. It is dominated by grant seekers who support the myth to perpetuate their revenue and academic careers. This movement is led by civil servants, politicians

---

[39] Judith Curry, "Why I Don't Believe in Science," in *Climate, Etc.* https://judithcurry.com/2019/03/26/why-i-dont-believe-in-science/.

and media requesting that the masses do as they say, as they know better as to their welfare. This is going on in the name of correcting global warming. Increased taxation and fattening academia will not change the climate. The United Nations will continue its crusade, but it will continue to be based on political advocacy rather than factual science. Prosperity > poverty!

The United Nations' Intergovernmental Panel on Climate Change (IPCC) is and has been the major driving force on putting forth the climate change agenda. There have been five sequences of reports. Each has become more aggressive and rigid with time and consensus that the issue is settled. The first flaw is that they produce scientific working group reports of 300–400 pages in which the limitations of the data, hypothesis and uncertainties are acknowledged. Generated from these reports are something called Summary for Policy Makers. The media and politicians do not read 300–400 page reports. The IPCC policy summaries simplify out limitations and uncertainties while adding a political spin of the urgency of the matter.[40]

A group of 500 prominent scientists and professionals were so fed up by the IPCC's continual misuse of pseudoscience for political self-serving goals that they wrote a registered letter to the United Nations Secretary-General titled "The European Climate

---

[40] Donna Laframboise, *The Delinquent Teenager Who Was Mistaken for the World's Top Climate Expert: IPCC Expose* (Toronto: Ivy Avenue Press, 2011).

Declaration." The list of signees was led by CLINTEL (Climate Intelligence Foundation) cofounder Professor Guus Berkhout. It calls for a wider range of input to the climate debate. It further states that there is no climate emergency. Current climate models on which international policies are being based are unfit for that purpose. Policies should be designed to benefit people and are instead destroying their economic well-being. Trillions of dollars are being squandered on the basis of immature and distorted models. They advocate instead a policy based on sound science and economics. Mitigation attempts have been costly and often unnecessary.

Their points were as follows:

1. Natural as well as anthropogenic factors cause warming.
2. Warming is far slower than predicted.
3. Climate policy relies on inadequate models.
4. Carbon dioxide is not a pollutant. It is a plant food that is essential to all life on Earth. Photosynthesis is a blessing. More CO_2 is beneficial for nature, for greening the earth: additional CO_2 in the air has promoted growth in global plant biomass. It is also good for agriculture, increasing the yields of crops worldwide.
5. Global warming has not increased natural disasters.

6. Climate policy must respect scientific and economic realities.
7. There is no climate emergency. Therefore, there is no cause for panic.[41]

There is no evidence from observational scientists that climate sensitivity of 2–4 °C will lead to a doubling of atmospheric CO_2. It has been inferred, based on speculation. This was confirmed by the 33-year period of (slight) global cooling that took place between 1942 and 1975 as CO_2 emissions increased by 425%! This has been confirmed again by the fact that the 50% increase in CO_2 emissions has not resulted in any net warming in the past 22 years. This stasis in global temperature rise is stated in the 2013 report on climate models, and the hiatus in global mean surface warming.[42]

There are two sets of temperature data. One comes from ground measurements and the second from satellite measurements. Ground data is affected by readings with variable reliability ranging from local urban heat effect to technical issues with remote area reporting. Satellite data is more consistent and uniform. That satellite data from 1997 to 2019 shows a significant lack of or lull in

---

[41] "There Is No Climate Emergency, Say 500 Experts in Letter to the United Nation," Carpe Diem, https://www.aei.org/carpe-diem/there-is-no-climate-emergency-say-500-experts-in-letter-to-the-united-nations/.

[42] Gregory Flato and Jochem Marotzke, "Evaluation of Climate Models," https://www.ipcc.ch/site/assets/uploads/2018/02/WG1AR5_Chapter09_FINAL.pdf.

global warming. Climate change advocates struggle to explain this.

Professors Spencer and Christy are esteemed climatologists at the University of Alabama. They are the key scientists responsible for maintaining the National Aeronautics and Space Administration (NASA) satellite temperature record. This prestigious organization is considered the largest holder of uniform worldwide undisputable factual temperature data.[43] Their assertion of "no significant temperature increase" is solid fact. Their statement that alarmist climate theory does not match the factual observations has to be taken more seriously than current media, political and United Nations propaganda. Biologist Thomas Huxley philosophically would have stated that the hypothesis is slain by the ugly facts. The possibility that climate change is currently being caused by Industrial Age humans is discounted by the fact that every current climate range and variation has been seen before.

With scientific measurements, there is always a required margin of error. A footlong ruler cannot measure microns. The problem with climate change is that alarm is being sounded about 0.5–2.0° C increases when the margin of measurement error in the data is far greater than that. Quantities of concern have been in the realm of 0.7 degrees per century. Temperature

---

[43] Roy Spencer, Climate Confusion: How Global Warming Hysteria Leads to Bad Science, Pandering Politicians and Misguided Policies That Hurt the Poor (New York: Encounter Books, 2008).

ranges on a regular day in a city such as Calgary can be -10 degrees to +5. With Chinooks, the range can be double or triple that. Science is the observation of facts and events that stay consistent every time they are observed.

Weather is not climate. Weather varies from summer to winter within a spectrum of -40° C to +40° C. The range from north to south geographically at any one time is similar. It varies place to place, year to year. It varies with El Niño, La Niña, ocean currents and sunspots. Any trend line is a positioning along points of highly variable data.

The amount of global temperature cooling or warming is based upon normalization to the average of the period 1961 to 1990. This arbitrary bench line itself is somewhat dishonest, as it starts in the 1942 -1975 period of global cooling. The IPCC itself quotes a temperature rise from 1850 to 2010 of net 0.8° C.[44] Disastrous model predictions designed to create alarm have not occurred. This has been happening since the 1920s but reached a torrent in the 1990s and early 2000s. Why people and governments continue to believe in the game is difficult to comprehend.

The IPCC and their emotional promoters such as Al Gore and David Suzuki postulate most of their alarmism from graphs rather than actual data. The most extreme was the Michael Mann hockey stick

---

[44] Mark Handel and James Risbey, *Reflections on More than a Century of Climate Change Research*, <u>Climatic Change</u> volume 21, (1992).

graph, which ignored both the 500 to 1100 medieval warming period and the 1400 to 1700 little Ice Age. One has to look at the history of the Vikings. In their voyages during the first of these time periods, they used the term "Vineland" to refer to Greenland and Newfoundland. Greenland at that time had a more than subsistence agricultural base.

Dr. Tim Ball, in his book *The Deliberate Corruption of Climate Science,* challenged Mann's hockey stick graph. It distorted historical temperature data, and the exaggerated upward curved end had no foundation. Professor Mann took Dr. Ball to court and lost.[45] The Al Gore movie *An Inconvenient Truth* was a mockery of science. It involved gross exaggeration and distortion of facts. He sadly made a fortune from his deceptive, emotional and fearmongering diatribe. It was adopted by far too many educational agencies to support the myth.

Carbon dioxide is not a pollutant; it is part of nature's cycle. Trees and plants use it in photosynthesis to create oxygen. Nonetheless, the amount of CO_2 in the atmosphere is minor. It is currently thought to be .04%, up from .01% in the mid-nineteenth century (miniscule). One has to be aware that this type of change can be quoted as a fourfold increase even though it is minor in magnitude. There is much discussion as to even how much of that is anthropogenic. Greenhouses

---

[45] Tim Ball, *The Deliberate Corruption of Climate Science* (Apache Junction, AZ: Stairway Press 2014).

in Canada, whether they grow marijuana or vegetables, inject CO_2 to increase growth and production. In the last few years of carbon dioxide increase, there has been no corresponding increase in temperature. It is postulated by some that a global increase in CO_2 would create a positive greening of the earth.

Dr. Patrick Moore states that we are geologically in the Holocene, the second epoch of the Quaternary period. The planet has been warming since the Pleistocene, the last Ice Age 11,700 years ago. There were no automobiles, oil wells or coal plants 1,000 years ago. Dr. Moore is also troubled by the diatribe that humans are destroying nature and numerous species. Homo sapiens are a species and a success story of natural evolution. Species have evolved for millions of years. The Darwinian premise of survival of the fittest to reproduce is the wondrous process of nature by which organisms over the millennium have grown more complex, more efficient and more adaptive. In the process, species are left behind. The population of humankind and the level of development worldwide is growing rapidly. With agricultural management, humankind will evolve and even flourish. We are currently, with fertilizers and safe pesticides, obtaining five times our food production from the same amount of agricultural land.[46]

Dr. Moore has also made some astute observations

---

[46] Patrick More, *Confessions of a Greenpeace Dropout* (Beatty Street, 2010).

on CO_2 levels. In the Pleistocene, CO_2 levels were 85,000 parts per million (ppm). Greenhouse operators keep their CO_2 levels at 800 to 1200 ppm. Today's outdoor CO_2 level is 400 ppm, and in theory, the asphyxiating level for humans is 50,000 ppm. The navy maintains safe submarine levels at 8,000 ppm or less.

It is not possible for the average individual to observe complex climate factors personally, so we must listen somewhat to others in formulating our stance. The question is who. Dr. Moore has a PhD in ecology (the study of ecosystems and the environment). He grew up in the forestry industry and was part of a major environmental organization. Dr. Suzuki studied fruit flies. Al Gore was a defunct politician. Greta Thunberg is an inexperienced teenage high school student. Make your choice.

University of East Anglia professor Mike Hulme asserted, "Ask not what we can do for climate change but what climate change can do for us"[47] (i.e., how can it be used to further socialist goals of income redistribution and supposed sustainable development?). My favourite analogy is the watermelon: green on the outside, but pink to the core. This has been the political, media, IPCC, NGO and academic spin that has distorted factual science. The problem is that the IPCC in general did not approach the issue from the point of view of evaluating the issue but assumed it to be a fact and

---

[47] Mike Hulme, *Why We Disagree About Climate Change* (Cambridge University Press, 2009).

the task was how to support and promote the premise regardless of its validity. That is politics, not science. The University of East Anglia is the United Kingdom's centre for climate change and collection of related data. They have been caught and documented distorting historically higher temperature records to make the current temperatures appear irregularly high[48].

Prime Minister Margaret Thatcher was a big proponent of the global warming issue but dropped it when she observed the actual details and problems with the cause. The current Canadian government, with the same goal, has been accused of deleting climate data they deem to be unsupportive of their current climate hysteria. How can you have objective, valid science when you distort and misrepresent the data?

Insurance bureaus and statistics indicate no increase in extreme weather events. Vastly increased worldwide reporting of such events may make it appear so. The world has seen vast social and economic improvements. When it comes to issues such as global warming, one must assign priorities. There are far more immediate and concrete issues that deserve attention.[49] It is interesting to note that Bjorn was a statistician with multiple charts and factual data showing that the world has in the last decades made great progress in real issues related to air pollution, disease control and

---

[48] Donna Laframboise, The Delinquent Teenager Ivy Avenue Press 2011
[49] Bjorn Lomberg, *The Skeptical Environmentalist* (Cambridge University Press, 2001).

agricultural productivity. These real concrete issues should have a higher priority than theoretical climate change. These two facts were probable reasons as to why some of the climate crowd objected to his book being published.

Increased worldwide forest fires in California, the Amazon and Australia have been falsely attributed to climate change. The more likely cause is poor forest management. This can be a failure to clear fire-fuelling underbrush. It can also be attributed to preserving large sections of forest in the name of conservation. What is preserved are vast expanses of opportunity for major fires. In California and Okanogan, Canada, we have seen large incursions of urban housing projects into previous tracts of forest. This, more than climate, is probably the cause of increased fire-related financial and human losses. The same could be said for the urbanization of storm-prone coastal areas and flood plains.

Dr. Willie Soon is an astrophysicist and aerospace engineer employed as a researcher at the Solar and Stellar Physics Division of the Harvard Smithsonian Centre for Astrophysics. It is his contention that the climate is more affected by changes in the sun's cycles and sunspots than any other factor. However, factors are many and complex. Carbon dioxide is the food of life and not a culprit in climate change. Sunspot activity on the sun follows a little understood 11-year cycle. Activity rises and falls, creating the so-called solar maximum and then the solar minimum. During a solar maximum, the sun has more sunspots. Conversely, when the sun enters a solar minimum as of two years ago, the energy from the sun lessens. From 1650 to 1710, temperatures across much of the Northern Hemisphere plunged when the sun entered a quiet phase now called the Maunder Minimum.[50]

Climate change, it has to be stated again, is being used as a *weapon* both to lead us to world socialism and as a blatant tax grab. It is not a noble cause to save the planet. The phrase climate denier is used to slur anyone who dares discuss opposition. As stated before that is an offense to all who died in that tragedy. China continues to build coal power plants at a rate of hundreds per year. Germany, once the proclaimed leader of wind and solar energy, has had to return to coal. In addition to being unreliable, wind power is not the great renewable it was postured to be.

Companies are searching for ways to deal with the tens of thousands of wind turbine blades that have reached the end of their lives. In the United States alone, about 8,000 will be removed in each of the next four years. They are not recyclable.[51]

---

[50] Sean Martin, "Weather Warning: Earth May Be Hit by Mini Ice Age As Sun 'Hibernates,'" Climate Change Dispatch, February 2020, https://climatechangedispatch.com/earth-mini-ice-age-sun-hibernates/.
[51] Chris Martin, "Wind Turbine Blades Can't Be Recycled, So They're Piling up in Landfills," *Bloomburg Green*, https://www.bloomberg.com/news/features/2020-02-05/wind-turbine-blades-can-t-be-recycled-so-they-re-piling-up-in-landfills.

Catherine Mckenna was designated the Minister of Climate Change and the Environment in Justin Trudeau's cabinet. Climate change is a hyped cause being used for political purposes. The actual environment is a real issue. Clean water and air are vital to our health and well-being as a community and country. That is the real environmental issue. Ironically, people who work in the resource industry on infrastructure projects and development are in contact with our great and vast land on a daily basis. They have a greater appreciation, knowledge and concern than distant urbanites thinking great and restrictive thoughts based on irrelevant, idealistic dogma. Catherine was in a science-based portfolio without any science background or even familiarity, let alone understanding. Sadly, the funding and attention went to the political issue climate change and not the real issue, the environment.

More than 205 billion litres of sewage and wastewater spew into Canada's rivers and oceans annually. Sewage does not have the same glamorous ring as much-hyped climate change. In 2015, Newfoundland and Labrador dumped 10.6 billion litres of raw sewage into oceans and rivers. BC dumped 82 billion litres in 2015. Manitoba dumped 12.5 and Nova Scotia 9.4. The climate change focus distracts from this real problem.[52]

In November 2018, with the approval of Environment Minister Catherine McKenna, Montreal dumped eight billion litres of raw sewage into the St. Lawrence River over several days.[53] The focus was on the wrong cause and the wrong priority!

In summary, these are the weaknesses of the climate weapon:

- It is carbon dioxide, not carbon.
- CO_2 is necessary for plant growth; it is not a pollutant.
- Photosynthesis converts CO_2 into oxygen.
- Greenhouses maintain CO_2 levels two times current atmosphere.
- Science is a process (Facts > Logic > Conclusion).
- It is not a belief or rigid final authority.
- 97% of scientists say it is a myth from a limited, biased survey.
- NASA satelite data shows no warming for 20 years.

---

[52] Elizabeth Thomson, "Billions of Litres of Raw Sewage, Untreated Wastewater Pouring into Canadian Waterways," *CBC News*, December 2016, https://www.cbc.ca/news/politics/sewage-pollution-wastewater-cities-1.3889072.

[53] Rene Bruemmer, "Eight Billion Litres of Raw Sewage Dumped into the St. Lawrence River," *Montreal Gazette*, November 2018,
https://montrealgazette.com/news/local-news/city-to-begin-massive-sewage-dump-wednesday.

- Predictictions of global disaster have not occurred.
- Cherry-picked models ignored the medieval warming and Little Ice Age.
- The 1–2° C scare factor is arbitrary and proabaly unmeasureable.
- The influence of suncycles and clouds is not addressed.
- Real environmental issues (i.e., dumping raw sewage) have been ignored.

The climate weapon is being used by Prime Minister Trudeau to thwart the Western Canadian oil and gas industry and increase government power in Ottawa. The industry and economic reality are being needlessly sacrificed for a weak theoretical concept. The supposed cause of less oil consumption is exposed by the fact that during Mr. Trudeau's reign, Canadian imports of oil from Saudi Arabia have increased 66%[54]. Again, the concern is that our prosperity is in peril.

---

[54] Chris Arsenault, Canada's oil imports from Saudi Arabia on the rise since 2014, April 2019. https://www.cbc.ca/news/business/saudi-oil-imports-rise-canada-diplomacy-1.5096887

CHAPTER 8

Political Disaster Returns

In November 2015, Justin Junior Trudeau was elected prime minister of Canada. Some of his career background includes having been a camp counsellor, a night club bouncer, a snowboard instructor and a substitute drama teacher. In all fairness, he did acquire a degree in literature from McGill and an education degree from the University of British Columbia. As a Member of Parliament, he represented a Montreal urban riding team. His main qualification for prime minister was the very well-known Trudeau family name. His understanding of or concern for economic and financial issues was, to say the least, weak.

Much of his backing and campaign funding would appear to have come from the big Quebec business firms of Bombardier and SNC-Lavalin. The heavy ties of SNC-Lavalin to rich contracts with the Saudi Arabian oil industry would cloud many of his decisions with regard to the Canadian domestic oil industry and domestic pipelines. It could also explain why absurdly domestic crude has a carbon tax and Saudi Arabian crude does not.

The Federal Court of Appeal in June 2016 overturned the 2014 positive decision of the Harper Government with regard to the Northern Gateway Pipeline.[55] It sent the Joint Review Panel's recommendation back to Trudeau for reconsideration.

In July 2016, Trudeau and the Liberal government of Canada directed the National Energy Board to dismiss the Northern Gateway Pipeline Project.[56] The Liberal government and Trudeau determined that the project was not in the public interest because it would result in crude oil tankers transiting through the sensitive ecosystem of the Douglas channel and the Great Bear Rainforest. The Spirit Bear occupied a very small portion of the area. Therefore it was not relevant.

In making this decision, the government supposedly considered the Joint Review Panel, the views of Indigenous people, concerned unaffected Canadians

---

[55] John Paul Tasker, "Ottawa Won't Appeal a Court Decision Blocking Northern Gateway Pipeline," *CBC News*, September 2016, https://www.cbc.ca/news/politics/enbridge-northern-gateway-federal-court-1.3770543.

[56] Mike De Souza, "Trudeau Approves Kinder Morgan Pipeline, Rejects One of Two Enbridge Projects," *National Observer*, November 2016, https://www.nationalobserver.com/2016/11/29/news/breaking-trudeau-approves-kinder-morgan-pipeline-rejects-one-two-enbridge-projects.

and the orders of the Federal Court of Appeal. The government also cited that in their political opinion, the pipeline would in general cause unjustified environmental effects. One more strongly suspects that the Liberal government and Trudeau sentiment was that if the Harper government approved it, they opposed it. Again, decisions made from afar and based on dogma trump the well-being of local communities. One also suspects that the Saudi Arabian SNC-Lavalin connection had something to do with the downgrading of a competitive Canadian oil Industry. Again we see Trudeau virtue signalling to hide self-serving actions.

The Joint Review Panel had been established by the previous Minister of the Environment and the Chair of the National Energy Board in January 2010. Its report was submitted in December 2013. It was the summation of three and a half years of extensive research and indigenous consultation by highly qualified experts. It thoroughly considered along with economic merits the environmental concerns cited by the current government. Indigenous consultation showed the majority of the bands actually along the route were in favour of and looking forward to opportunities that would come therefrom. Nonetheless, political whim and misjudgement killed the project.

To further cement the end of this viable project, the Trudeau government put forward a blanket ban against crude oil tankers on the North Coast of British Columbia. The ban would extend from the Alaskan border to the north of Vancouver Island. The Bill was officially put forward by Liberal Minister of Transport Marc Garneau. This proposal would subsequently become Bill C-48, The Oil Tanker Moratorium Act. It was, with a Liberal majority, passed by the House of Commons in 2018. No input was accepted from industry. The bill proceeded to the Canadian Senate in May 2018. Nothing in the government of Canada proceeds rapidly.

The Senate transport committee reviewed the matter extensively. It presented a well thought through report. The report recommended that the Bill be defeated. The Bill was presented to the Senate as a whole. The report had expressed concerns that it could cause further economic concerns to Alberta and Saskatchewan. The Liberal government, in addition to having a majority in the House of Commons, also controlled the Senate. The bill was passed 53–38.[57]

There was no such ban on the St. Lawrence River into Montreal or the East Coast. Oil tankers regularly delivered foreign crude oil to refineries in Montreal and New Brunswick. Much of that crude oil came from Saudi Arabia. Tankers carrying crude oil from Alaska to more southern US ports regularly transited the same waters adjacent to the British Columbia North Coast. Nonetheless, Bill C-48 passed.

---

[57] Rebecca Joseph, "Tanker Ban Bill: What It Means, Who Is For and Against It and What's Next," June 2019,
https://globalnews.ca/news/5365808/tanker-ban-bill-questions/.

Much of the Trudeau Green agenda and the strangling of the Western Canadian oil and gas industry comes from the virtue-signalling premise that the age of fossil fuels is to be replaced by wind, solar and other carbon-free fuels. Yet since the Trudeau regime came to power, imports of Saudi Arabian crude oil into Quebec and New Brunswick have increased by 66%. Could this possibly be because of the SNC-Lavalin overwhelming contracts with the Saudi Arabian oil industry? Perhaps it is just that Mr. Trudeau and the Laurentian elite have a stronger loyalty to Saudi Arabia and the Arab world than to Western Canada.

The First Nations Financial Transparency Act was enacted by the Stephen Harper Conservative Government. The purpose of this act was to enhance the financial accountability and transparency of First Nations by requiring the preparation and public disclosure of their consolidated financial statements. This was a vitally needed piece of legislation. The legislation was correct in its purpose in that it was to defend indigenous people from leaders who were not acting in the best interest of their people.

Just after its election in November 2015, the Trudeau government issued a statement via the Minister of Indigenous and Northern Affairs regarding the First Nations Financial Transparency Act. It proclaimed that henceforth it has stopped all discretionary compliance measures related to the First Nations Financial Transparency Act. It was reinstating funding withheld from First Nations under these measures. It was suspending any court actions against First Nations who have not complied with the act.[58] A giant step backward, to say the least. Was this part of Mr. Trudeau showing solidarity with hereditary chiefs and their automatic entitlement, corrupt or not? That is something he could more readily identify with than people's basic rights, coming from that route himself. No, I think if former Prime Minister Harper did it, then he opposed it.

This, perhaps more indirectly than directly, influenced development on and around indigenous land. Earned money versus government money. Leaders' money in the pocket versus real progress for the people. Prosperity in peril.

Let's go on to issues less specific and more to do with impression and image. Canada has had for decades a prestigious international image. In early 2018, Prime Minister Trudeau made a trip to India. The Canadian High Commissioner invited a Sikh extremist named Jaspal Atwal to a dinner in Delhi. He had a murder conviction on his record and had been found guilty of trying to kill an Indian cabinet minister. Perhaps visually more serious were the international videos of Trudeau and his family dancing around like minstrels in ridiculous Bollywood-type costumes. A trip that was

---

[58] David Akin, "Fewer First Nations Disclosed Financial Data After PM Suspended Key Accountability Measure," *National Post*, January 2017, https://nationalpost.com/news/politics/first-nations-fiscal-accountability-dropped-after-liberals-cut-enforcement-measure-at-end-of-2015.

supposed to cement Canadian-Indian relations totally embarrassed and offended the classier Indian Prime Minister Narendra Modi.[59]

Marijuana was one of Prime Minister Trudeau's wondrous campaign promises. It got him a lot of votes, not totally but especially among millennial voters. Marijuana use was as widespread as alcohol and perhaps less harmful. The legalization was approved in the fall of 2018. That was a good thing but threw out the possibility that Canada could, instead of being a world energy power, be a global drug dealer.

Debt was another major issue. The Harper government, with considerable effort, had brought not the debt but the deficit and net government spending to zero. Trudeau had been elected on a campaign of moderate deficits. Trudeau skyrocketed debt. Questionable loans to Trudeau backer Bombardier and gifts to profitable large corporations such as Canadian Tire and Loblaws were part of the problem. Worse were uncontrolled overseas third-world grants and outrageous funding for highly questionable illegal immigration.

The Harper Government, with its last term in office projected a 2015–16 financial year surplus of $1.4 billion. The newly elected Trudeau government in

---

[59] Barkha Duff, "Trudeau's India Trip Is a Total Disaster—and He Has Only Himself to Blame," The *Washington Post*, February 2018, https://www.washingtonpost.com/news/global-opinions/wp/2018/02/22/trudeaus-india-trip-is-a-total-disaster-and-he-has-himself-to-blame/.

October 2015, for the financial year 2015–16 ending in March, gave an actual small deficit of $1.0 billion. The 2016–17 financial year had a reported deficit of $17.8 billion. All of Trudeau's first four-year term had deficits in that range. This was in contrast to stated minor deficits. The Canadian federal debt in 2012 was $600 billion as opposed to $768 billion in 2018. The Finance Minister Bill Morneau has currently projected the 2019–20 deficit to be $19.8 billion. Also projected were deficits into the 2040s.[60] This is in contrast to this financially irresponsible government promising a balance in and from 2019 onward. Again, progress forward followed by progress backward.

Four major negations of previous progress include the cancellation of previously approved, needed northern infrastructure, indigenous responsibility downgraded, lost foreign image and renewed spiralling debt. The massive shift to climate hysteria and destruction of the highly productive Western Canadian energy sector has been discussed under our segment on climate change.

Some other puzzling incidents might be mentioned. This government has made virtue signalling comments about human rights and racism. Yet the prime minister himself was caught with racist minstrel portrayals. The energy industry was crucified with endless unfounded court delays. The prime minister proclaimed, "Let

---

[60] Erik Hertzberg, "Trudeau's Deficits Likely to Grow on Weakening Fiscal Outlook," BNN Bloomberg, November 2019, https://www.bnnbloomberg.ca/trudeau-s-deficits-likely-to-grow-on-weakening-fiscal-outlook.

justice take due process and get these projects done in the right way." Then he attempted to override his attorney general to corrupt the courts.

In 2019, the corruption and bribery scandal erupted around one of his favoured Quebec companies, SNC-Lavalin. It was charged in February 2015 by the RCMP and federal prosecutors with corruption and fraud for bribing the corrupt Libyan regime of Muammar al-Gaddafi to secure engineering contracts worth billions of dollars. Stephen Harper was the Conservative prime minister at that time. Prior to this, the Asian Development Bank had barred SNC from its contracts in 2004. In 2013, the World Bank had also banned SNC from bidding on contracts because of corrupt practices and bribery. The bribery was so extreme that it even involved a yacht and Canadian prostitutes for Gaddafi's son. Although Libya was the gigantic one, bribery was not limited thereto. It had also occurred with several other African countries. There were also allegations of domestic bribery in connection with a Montreal hospital construction.

The Trudeau Liberal SNC-Lavalin conspiracy was kicked off by a conversation between the SNC-Lavalin CEO Neil Bruce and the Finance Minister Bill Morneau at the World Economic Forum in Davos in 2018. SNC suggested or perhaps dictated to Morneau the concept of a deferred prosecution agreement (DPA). Up until this time, Canada did not have such legislation. SNC referred to this as a remediation agreement and actually delivered it to the Finance Minister's policy director, requesting timely implementation. The concept of a DPA was slipped into the 2018 omnibus Budget Bill. This was even though Trudeau had specifically called out Harper for using this approach. The bill and the DPA request by SNC was passed in June 2018.[61]

The Harper government as an anti-corruption tool had set up an act called the Director of Public Prosecutions. The then Conservative government set this up as an independent office to prosecute federal crimes. Ironically, it was inspired by Adscam, a previous scandal under the Chretien regime. This was a mess during the Quebec Referendum period whereby the Liberal government had set up a fund to promote federalism. It was a massive rip-off of supposed advertising monies being illegally diverted to dummy agencies and even the Liberal Party itself for inflated and even non-existent services.

In August of the same year, SNC complained to the Finance Minister's chief of staff that their bill had been passed but they were still facing charges. He then forwarded the complaint to the Chief of Staff of the Attorney General. She rightly stated that the office of the Director of Public Prosecutions is statutorily independent of government and that even asking for

---

[61] Mark Gollom, "What You Need to Know About the SNC-Lavalin Affair," *CBC News*, February 2019,
https://www.cbc.ca/news/politics/trudeau-wilson-raybould-attorney-general-snc-lavalin.

a status update may be improper political interference. Wanting to put a stop to SNC prosecution, Butts then told the Attorney General, "There is no solution here that doesn't involve some interference."[62] Gerald Butts was one of the key advisors to the Prime Minister. Prior to that he was head of the World Wildlife Fund where he diverted funds from protecting species to his personal political cause. He also crippled the Ontario economy with overpriced "Green" hydro. He and the prime minister did not like what they referred to as a Harper law. If you do not like a law, you can just not abide by it? The independent prosecutor's office decided that the deferred prosecution or remediation agreement that they had got put through did not apply to SNC-Lavalin.

In September 2018, the independent prosecutor's office informed Attorney General Jody Wilson-Raybould of their decision. The law allowed her, in theory, to overrule the Director of Public Prosecutions as unethical, as that may have been. Realizing the difficulty of the situation, she made a point of getting input from the ministry, the department and several former attorney-generals. In a mid-September meeting, Prime Minister Trudeau communicated to Attorney General Wilson-Raybould his dissatisfaction with her decision not to overrule the Director of Public Prosecutions. The head of the Privy Council, who

---

[62] Ezra Levant, The Libranos, Rebel News Network 2019

headed the whole civil service, conveyed to her similar intimidations. This was from a position that should have been politically neutral. Finance Minister Morneau proceeded to continually harass the Attorney General over the manner. Eventually the SNC-Lavalin chairman Kevin Lynch himself, via Scott Brison, joined the crowd of white men beating on. Wilson-Raybould. Scott Brison was a former left wing MP and part of the Trudeau inner circle. Intimidation continued and escalated from the Privy Council, assorted Liberal politicians and the SNC itself. In February 2019, Attorney General Jodi Wilson-Raybould resigned from the cabinet.[63]

This seemed to disagree with his virtuous statements of allowing courts independence with regard to petty, multiple and continual detrimental pipeline blockages. It seems to disagree with his much-touted virtue signalling about women's and aboriginal rights. He and his cohorts ran roughshod over a distinguished, educated, female aboriginal lawyer trying to do the right thing. She had been a regional chief of the BC Assembly of First Nations and chair of the First Nations Finance Authority. You would have thought that would have made her someone to be respected not only on justice

---

[63] Amanda Connoly, "Jody Wilson-Raybould Resigns from Cabinet amid SNC-Lavalin Affair, Trudeau Surprised and Disappointed," *Global News*, February 12, 2019, https://globalnews.ca/news/4952236/jody-wilson-raybould-resigns-snc-lavalin-affair/.

matters but more so on aboriginal matters. Women and aboriginals were there to be seen and not heard.

Yet with never-ending pomposity, Trudeau carries on with his "feminist" propaganda. Remember when he bragged that 50% women on his cabinet was more important than competency? In 2017, he attended the Woman in the World Summit in New York City and proclaimed, "Wherever I go, I sit down with leaders in business, particularly women, and ask what more can we do."

Later he announced he would donate $20 million of taxpayer money to a group called Woman Deliver because everyone benefits from a more gender-equal world.[64] It was easier to throw money at equality than act on it.

So how does this affect mega-infrastructure projects, Western Canada and the Canadian oil and gas industry? There is an established pattern of talk the walk and very little walk the talk. There is high moral talk of doing development the right way, of merging the fight for environmental concerns with responsible building of needed pipeline infrastructure. There is talk of doing due diligence and listening to the science. In Bill C-69, we see, included in due diligence, the giving of equal weight to folklore-based traditional aboriginal knowledge and modern science and engineering. Also to be included is the gender impact—whatever the

---

[64] "Justin Speaks at Women Deliver Conference," YouTube, June 2019, https://www.youtube.com/wA4a0q6lAp4.

hell that is. Concepts address the fact that he has little or no knowledge of business, economics or building anything.

Bill C-69, the "no more pipelines" bill, replaced the National Energy Board with something called the Impact Assessment Agency.[65] Perhaps this was even worse than Trudeau's Bill C-48, the Oil Tanker Moratorium Act. Bill C-69 replaced a body of qualified engineers, safety technicians, lawyers, biologists and other associated scientists, experts and professionals with mostly Laurentian elite lawyers and bureaucrats.

Appointed directors were

- Cassie Doyle, former senior civil servant with federal natural resources and Environment Canada;
- George Vegh, lawyer with McCarthy Tétrault and formerly with the Ontario Energy board;
- Alain Jolicour, member of the academic board of governors of the University of Ottawa and member of the NEB since 2016;
- Ellen Barry, former New Brunswick Minister of Tourism; and
- Melanie Debassage, bureaucrat, BC Assembly of First Nations.

---

[65] "What is Bill C-69? Context Energy Examined," https://context.capp.ca/energy-matters/2018/og101_what-is-bill-c69.

Appointed independent commissioners were

- Damien Cote, former NEB board member, formerly of the Inuvialuit Corporation;
- Kathy Penney, assessment review board, Rocky View county;
- Wilma Jackknife, lawyer for indigenous people;
- Stephanie Luciuk, academic Mount Royal College;
- Trena Grimoldby, lawyer, Alberta Insurance Council review board and three oil firms; and
- Mark Walton, lawyer with Stevenson Doell in Victoria.

None of them have any technical, engineering or scientific expertise. There is minimal to no industry representation,[66] just a lot of underemployed, high-salary former bureaucrats in need of a prestigious position and accompanying salary! Political patronage had to be a major factor.

Among other problems with the bill, as well as putting indigenous folklore on the same level as modern science and engineering, is that it adds general downstream or retail emissions as part of evaluating an unconnected upstream project. Responsible Industry input from those to be actually involved or with even practical experience seemed relatively non-existent.

---

[66] "Canadian Energy Regulator Replaces Venerable NEB" *The Roughneck*, 62, 6 (October 2019).

Probably the worst aspect was that it removed a step-by-step technical-evaluation process that can be followed by a project proponent to get approval. It replaces this with decision by political whim, possibility for bias, favouritism and even bribery. It effectively discourages any rational, financially responsible business corporation from putting forth a project for approval. One wonders if appointees to the agency will still be paid when there are no proposed projects to approve or reject.

In the October 2019 election, this prime minister and the Liberal government were returned to power. That is again prosperity in peril.

In February 2020, the obstruction and the idiocy continued as we saw the Teck Frontier oil sands project brought into dispute. It was a project totally within Alberta and should not have been subject to federal intrusion. Area First Nations communities had been consulted and were onside. They were looking forward to new employment and contracting opportunities. The project had gone through a multiyear process of step-by-step evaluation by a joint federal provincial review panel consisting of technically qualified professionals and was deemed to be socioeconomically in national interest. Mr. Trudeau and Mr. Morneau managed to intrude into this situation and ransomed approval of the project for support of their biased political agenda by imposing further never-ending conditions. Teck withdrew. The local indigenous communities and oil sands workers from Ft. Mac to Edmonton to Newfoundland lost. Alberta and Canada at large lost. Quebec, Trudeau and the green activists celebrated.

CHAPTER 9

Indigenous Issues

Indigenous people in Canada have been used as a "noble idea" pawn for far too long by people with their own self-focused agenda. It is time to defend the rights of indigenous people to say yes. For far too long, "environmental" activists, the federal government, the United Nations, the courts and even mainline Canadian churches have vehemently defended the rights of aboriginal communities to say no, to reject development on their lands.

They all had their own vested, self-focused interests. The eco-activist crowd wanted to keep development shut down no matter the socioeconomic cost. The current government wanted to keep the billions of dollars of annual indigenous bureaucracy in place. The United Nations wished to continue their crusade, however invalid and sanctimonious. The judiciary wanted to keep the never-ending power trip and legal bills flowing. The churches, with their socialist-bias self-righteousness opposed free enterprise development in general. None of these entities were really concerned about the individuals or their cause of having opportunities, jobs and prosperity.

This defending of the no and ignoring the yes has gone through at least three major infrastructure pipeline deliberations. The least remembered of these was the senior Trudeau/Justice Berger Mackenzie Valley fiasco. A three-year study was conducted to come up with a 10-year moratorium. The Inuit of Inuvik still have fond memories of their mid-seventies prosperity and say, "Wow! What happened?"

The Northern Gateway Pipeline was a 2010 proposed pipeline from the Bruderheim Alberta to Kitimat British Columbia. Its prime goal was to get Alberta oil sands to a Pacific coast port and access to world markets. It offered major development and associated jobs and opportunity to both the indigenous and non-indigenous residents of Northern British Columbia. The vast majority of the First Nations bands along the route and the residents of British Columbia were in favour of the project and were looking forward to the socioeconomic benefits it would bring.

In 2014, Prime Minister Stephen Harper approved the project. In 2015, Prime Minister Trudeau cancelled the project.

In the aftermath of this death knell from afar, many indigenous leaders expressed anger and disappointment, in particular Elmer Ghostkeeper of the Buffalo Lake Metis Settlement, Chief Elmer Derrick of the Gitxsan Nation and Dale Swampy of the Samson Cree. Ghostkeeper summarized that more than 30 of the 42 bands along the proposed route had been looking forward to sharing in the construction jobs and ongoing long-term benefits that the project would have facilitated.[67] It is hard for any project anywhere to have 100% support,[68] but they were back to the dependency on indigenous affairs handouts and welfare. Perhaps that was what the bureaucracy-based Liberal government really wanted to return to.

The First Nations Financial Transparency Act was enacted by the Stephen Harper Conservative government. The purpose of this act was to enhance the financial accountability and transparency of First Nations by requiring the preparation and public disclosure of their consolidated financial statements. It also required the schedules of remuneration paid and expenses reimbursed to a First Nation's chief and each of its councillors, acting in their capacity as such and in any other capacity, including their personal capacity

---

[67] Claudia Cattaneo, "We Are Very Disappointed: Loss of Northern Gateway Devastating for Many First Nations, Chiefs Say," *Financial Post*, April 2017, https://business.financialpost.com/commodities/energy/we-are-very-disappointed-loss-of-northern-gateway-devastating-for-many-first-nations-chiefs-say.

[68]

and by any entity that, in generally accepted accounting principles, is required to be consolidated with the First Nations.[69]

This was a vitally needed piece of legislation from multiple points of view. The federal government, via the Department of Indigenous Affairs, had for decades been dispensing billions of dollars to First Nations leaders with zero accounting. There was no consideration whatsoever as to whether or not these dollars were going to the purpose for which they were supposedly intended. Far too often the tribal chiefs and family member councillors used indigenous affairs dollars to enhance their own personal wealth and privilege. Elaborate Las Vegas vacations and international junkets, among other things, were indulged in by the chosen few. Salaries were paid out at an inflated rate far exceeding those of senior corporate executives and government officials. This was a rip off of the Canadian taxpayer. Far worse was the fact that the majority on many reserves did not have adequate clean water, education, housing, needed heating and food supplies. The reason was not that funding was not there. It was there, but it was being misused—or more specifically, stolen.

Don't get me wrong. Neither my comments nor the legislation were meant to target all indigenous leaders or people. The legislation's purpose was to defend indigenous people from corrupt leaders, those

---

[69] "First Nations Financial Transparency Act," https://laws-lois.justice.gc.ca/eng/acts/f-11.66/page-1.html.

who weren't acting in the interest of the people they supposedly led and represented. The Act was a step forward in returning power to the people, rewarding those who were championing progress and exposing those who were only gaming the system. This was moving forward. It was not so much an action to regulate indigenous people or even their leaders as it was a window to allow indigenous individuals to be aware of and defend their own governance.

The Trudeau government, just after its election in November 2015, issued a statement in December 2015 via the Minister of Indigenous and Northern Affairs concerning the First Nations Financial Transparency Act (FNFTA). It proclaimed that henceforth it had stopped all discretionary compliance measures related to the FNFTA. It was reinstating funding withheld from First Nations under these measures. It is suspending any court actions against First Nations who have not complied with the act. This was a major insult to indigenous leaders with integrity and a pat on the back to those who acted without integrity.

The following are two strong leaders of their people and Western Canadian energy as a whole.

Chief Jim Boucher, from the Fort McKay First Nation, is one of the great indigenous leaders. He was named 2018 Canadian Energy Person of the Year for his work developing the Fort McKay First Nation's successful oil and gas businesses. Boucher chairs the Fort McKay Group of Companies, which earned an average gross annual revenue of $1.7 billion in the last five years. The Fort McKay First Nation, with only 800 members, is a major oil sands contractor. It has no unemployment and an annual per capita income of $73,500.[70] The band shares its opportunities with other bands. Chief Boucher and his people are a credit to their community and country.

Joe Dion, CEO of Frog Lake Energy Resources and former Grand Chief of Alberta, is another indigenous leader of stature. Historically he was chief of the Kehewin Cree Nation in northeastern Alberta. He has spent decades promoting indigenous rights and opportunities in Western Canada. The company he leads is wholly owned by the Frog Lake First Nation. Joe and his group have shown and express how resource development can be a tool to build indigenous prosperity.[71]

In addition to support for the pipeline expansion, there is in the indigenous community, a significant and growing movement to acquire and become part of the pipeline ownership. Of the three groups interested in this, the earliest and most significant is the Western Indigenous Pipeline group. It is an entity representing the 55 First Nations along the pipeline route. They are looking at acquiring a 51% interest in the pipeline and the expansion project.

The group is led by Chief Michael LeBourdais of

---

[70] Ibid.
[71] Frog Lake Energy Resources, https://www.flerc.com/joe-dion-ucp-convention-red-deer-alberta/.

the Whispering Pines/Clinton Indigenous Band near Kamloops, British Columbia. He affirms that the existing pipeline goes right through his reserve and they've never had major issues. He states, "We're the ones most familiar with how the pipeline operates. We're the most familiar with the operations staff that are out here all the time."

He further expresses that pipelines generate solid revenue. With revenue from this project, he proudly states his band can build their own schools, hospitals and roads instead of being dependant on indigenous affairs government welfare. They would be proudly and truly independent.[72]

The Trans Mountain, aside two other issues, seem to have come to the plate. One is the new Teck Frontier oil sands project. It was within Alberta and as such should not have needed federal approval. The Teck Frontier oil sands project was brought into public dispute in February 2020. First Nations communities, Athabasca Chipewyan and Fort McKay, had been consulted and were onside. They would have been looking forward to the new employment and contracting opportunities. The project had gone through a multiyear process of step-by-step evaluation by technically qualified professionals.

On February 23, Teck president and CEO Don

---

[72] Randy Shore, "First Nations Seek Influence in Trans Mountain Pipeline Purchase," *Vancouver Sun*, May 2019, https://vancouversun.com/news/local-news/first-nations-seek-influence-and-control-in-pipeline-purchase.

Lindsay announced that they would be withdrawing from further application for environmental approval for their Frontier oil sands project He stated: "Teck put forward a socially and environmentally responsible project that was industry leading and had the potential to create significant economic benefits for Canadians. Frontier has unprecedented support from Indigenous communities and was deemed to be in the public interest by a joint federal-provincial review panel following weeks of public hearings and a lengthy regulatory process."[73]

Nonetheless, the Trudeau government, with absolute power and political whim, dictated that the project would not proceed without further jumping through never-ending hoops. Teck was forced to resolve that there was no constructive path forward for the project. Indigenous people and Canada lost again.

Secondly, the indigenous-approved Coastal Gas Link pipeline seems to have been brought back into public controversy by outside, unconnected paid protesters. We are seeing, in early 2020, a massive eruption of demonstrations to defend the rights of the Wet'suwet'en people. Where is this coming from? Rail lines are being blocked on Toronto-Montreal passenger trains. Trains north from Toronto to Barrie are being blocked. Prairie farmers cannot get their

---

[73] Don Lindsay, CEO Teck Resources, https://www.teck.com/media/Don-Lindsay-letter-to-Minister-Wilkinson.pdf.

crop to market. The BC Legislature in Victoria is being picketed.

The Coastal Gas Link pipeline from Northeast BC to Kitimat has been approved and is under construction. Thousands of indigenous workers have good paying jobs, some for the first time. The democratically elected chief and the democratically elected council of the Wet'suwet'en First Nation are supportive of and have signed agreements with the pipeline builder.[74] They will receive benefits to fund schools, recreational and medical facilities. The issue has been resolved. Not only that band, but every single one along the route has supported and signed benefit agreements with the pipeline builder. These agreements under case law support rather than diminish tribal land claims.

So what is going on? Pacific Gas and Electric in California has been buying BC natural gas for decades. Currently with the landlocked status, gas has an uneconomically low price. With an LNG pipeline and an alternative market, that price could increase significantly. Researcher and writer Vivian Krause has documented US interference in and enabling blocking of Canadian infrastructure. Is that what's going on? Why the sudden explosion of protests? Did leaders

---

[74] Laurie Hamelin, "Hereditary Chief in BC Says Community Needs LNG Pipeline," APTN News, December 2018, https://aptnnews.ca/2018/12/21/hereditary-chief-in-b-c-says-community-needs-lng-pipeline/.

of these activities get funded for one last-ditch effort? Our ineffectual socialist prime minister allows or dictates that the chaos continues. It benefits his non-development agenda. Would the RCMP without that bought political control not just enforce the law. Why do provincial premiers and police forces not enforce the law and remove the illegal blockades that do not even represent the indigenous group they claim to be part of? Some angry hereditary chiefs may be present. but they do not represent the people. The indigenous people of the Wet'suwet'en and other involved BC bands want foreigners and easterners to butt out of their affairs. They are intelligent and entitled to steer their own ships. A Wet'suwet'en woman says people in her community who have spoken up in support of this pipeline project in BC have been bullied and called traitors.[75] All 20 elected chiefs and elected band councils along the pipeline route, including Wet'suwet'en councils, have signed benefits agreements with Coastal GasLink. Is Canada a democracy or not? There's quite a bit of support for this project. But people are afraid to speak up because, in the past few years, people that have spoken up were either ostracized, ridiculed, bullied, harassed, threatened and been called a traitor—a sell-out.

---

[75] Bonnie George, "People Are Afraid to Speak Up: Wet'suwet'en Defends Her Support for Pipeline," February 2020, https://www.cbc.ca/radio/asithappens/as-it-happens-tuesday-edition.

Even a hereditary chief in British Columbia says people standing in the way of the LNG pipeline need to step aside and let the project get up and running. "I'm just getting tired of hearing about it," she says. "I'm just waiting for the shovel to get into the ground; let's get on with our lives," says Helen Michelle. Michelle has been a hereditary chief for 43 years[76].

Too often the old hereditary non-democratic chief system has been laden with corruption. JL Seagull tells a story of the system destroyed her family and their business.[77] Mr. Trudeau likes the chaos and fictitious concern more than the actual local community. Premiers such as Doug Ford have provincial police forces independent from Trudeau, and they can but are not acting to disperse this illegal action against their society.

Haisla First Nation chief councillor Crystal Smith has stated campaigns dating back to the 1990s by environmental protesters have shown a double standard that exists in the activist community, once again on full display in Wet'suwet'en territory regarding the Coastal GasLink pipeline. They had no concern about the poverty levels that our people were experiencing; there was no concern about the employment. Investing

---

[76] Laurie Hamelin, "Hereditary chief in BC says community needs LNG pipeline" https://aptnnews.ca/2018/12/21/hereditary-chief-in-b-c-says-community-needs-lng-pipeline/
[77] J. S. Seagull, "Wolves in Fancy Blankets," February 2020, https://www.jlsreport.com/2020/02/16/wolves-in-fancy-blankets/.

in ourselves is not selling out. Investing in our northern First Nations communities is not selling out.[78] Time to defend the right of indigenous people to say yes. Time to keep prosperity from peril.

---

[78] Gregory John, "Haisla Nation Chief Councillor Crystal Smith No Stranger to Double Standard from Activists," *Energy Now Media*, February 2020, https://energynow.ca/2020/02/haisla-nation-chief-councillor-crystal-smith-no-stranger-to-double-standard-from-activists/.

CHAPTER 10

Trans Mountain Pipeline and Expansion Project

This project is the most recent and most publicized example of turning prosperity into peril.

In March 1951, the Trans Mountain Oil Pipeline Company was established under an act of Parliament. Construction of the 1,150-kilometre pipeline began in 1952. The first oil flowed through the pipeline in October 1953 to the terminal at Burnaby, BC. This was a momentous, historical achievement, the first Canadian crude oil flowing from Edmonton, Alberta, to the British Columbia coast. The time involved from initiation through construction until initial production was two and a half years. No judicial hurdles. The initial production was 150,000 barrels of oil per day.

By 1957, the capacity had increased to 250,000 barrels per day.

In 1994, Terasen Pipelines acquired ownership of the Trans Mountain Pipeline Company Ltd. In 2005, Kinder Morgan acquired Terasen Pipelines. The pipeline in 2008, under Kinder Morgan, was upgraded to 300,000 barrels per day. This involved 160 kilometres of new pipeline between Hinton, Alberta, and Hargreaves, BC, along with 13 new pumping stations. Again there seemed to be no circus.

In February 2012, Kinder Morgan said it wanted to expand the Trans Mountain Pipeline to facilitate producers and shippers. The existing pipeline had been supplying oil and gas to the Vancouver mainland and Washington State since 1953. In those years, there were no major oil spills or marine accidents.[79]

What was the Kinder Morgan Expansion Project? The twinning of the existing 1,150-kilometre pipeline between Strathcona County (Edmonton), Alberta, and Burnaby, BC. It would increase flowthrough capacity from 300,000 to 890,000 barrels per day. The expansion would follow 73% of the original route. One would think, in theory, that much of the approval and permitting should be straightforward. Sadly, not so. In January 2013, Kinder Morgan signed long-term agreements with committed shippers for its increased capacity to 890,000 barrels per day. In May of that year,

---

[79] "Trans Mountain: Our History," https://www.transmountain.com/history.

the NEB (National Energy Board) approved the toll application for the expansion. The more major facilities application was made to the NEB.

The Trans Mountain Pipeline had been a proven and reliable source of transportation and home-heating supplies for multiple generations. Construction was planned for 2017 with the aim of having needed oil and natural gas flow through the line by 2019. This was partly to service expanding lower mainland demand and partly for product export.

People are emphatically yelling and screaming about things they barely know or understand. The problem is that they want the comforts of home heating and ease of transportation while spitting on that and those that provide it. People incoherently blocking this valid building of needed infrastructure are given a slap on the wrist and absolution at the same time jobs, economic prosperity and the supply of needed economic product go down the toilet. The circus begins.

In August 2015, the NEB postponed hearings on factual data because a contributor changed employers. In January 2016, Alberta NDP Premier Rachel Notley stated in a submission to the NEB that the Trans Mountain Pipeline expansion was in the best interests of Alberta and Canada. This she had to do as Premier of Alberta despite her NDP socialist dogma.

In January 2016, the federal government, under "save the world" Trudeau, said that pipeline projects would also now be assessed on greenhouse gas emissions.

This will be attached to both extraction processing and retail use. No such assessment will be applied to Quebec SNC-Lavalin oil imports from Trudeau-friendly Saudi Arabia.

Early in May 2016, the federal government appointed a three-member panel to conduct additional environmental review. In May 2016, the NEB concluded that the Trans Mountain Expansion Project is in the Canadian public interest and recommended the government approve the project, which Prime Minister Trudeau and the Liberal government did in June 2016. Attached were 157 conditions. In December 2016, the project received the necessary Certificate of Public Convenience and Necessity to permit construction and operation of the Trans Mountain Expansion. Four and a half years of expert evaluation and debate, but if it is done, it is done.

In January 2017, the British Columbia Environmental Assessment Office issued an environmental assessment certificate for the project. BC Premier Christy Clark gave her support for the project that would potentially generate billions of dollars for BC and Canadians. The absolutely fantastic deal for BC, Canadian taxpayers, investors and workers was coming together.

In May 2017, British Columbia municipalities and a minority of indigenous groups filed opposition to the project with the Federal Court of Appeal. This was happening although the NEB and other environmental assessment agencies spent some three to four years since

January 2013 addressing the issues and again raising concern. Extensive and detailed consultation had been made with all indigenous bands along the actual route and also with the two large bands on the adjacent coast. Environmental concerns along the route and in the nearby coastal waters were thoroughly addressed. Responses to remotely possible oil spills were also addressed—this, even though in the 59 years that the existing Trans Mountain Pipeline had been operating there had never been a marine oil spill. Whale sensitivity to potential tanker traffic noise would be less than that of current traffic of ferries, cruise ships and ocean cargo vessels.

The NEB expertise involved in this process was substantial. It included significant numbers of highly qualified lawyers, pipeline engineers, marine engineers, biologists, environmentalists, geoscientists, lawyers, safety experts and professional negotiators. There seemed to be some confusion or misassumption that the right to consult equated to a right of automatic refusal.

The indigenous bands in BC in general consist of two groups: those with significant wealth and prosperity, and those seeking opportunities, jobs and prosperity. This is particularly so relative to the general area of the Trans Mountain Pipeline. The haves seem undeterred from depriving the have-nots of their right to the same opportunities.

Two of the three major protesting bands are the Squamish and the Tsleil-Waututh, which are more on the coast than the actual route. They both have large holdings of Vancouver and North Vancouver real estate. Their level of wealth and prosperity allow them to be above the need for any further economic benefit. The other objecting band is the Coldwater near Merritt, BC. Their issue is a conflict about local water supply and the specific location of the pipeline expansion route. This can probably be addressed by local route alteration and additional protective measures.

The vast majority of bands along the route are supportive of the project, signed agreements and were looking forward to the jobs, opportunities and improved prosperity offered by the expansion. No major project anywhere can have 100% support. The key issue here is that the rights of a minority to say no or instil perpetual delay are overwhelming the rights of the vast majority to say yes.

Joe Dion, CEO of Frog Lake Energy Resources and former grand chief of Alberta, found from interviewing the bands along the Trans Mountain Expansion Route that 52 out 55 were in favour. That was overwhelming support.

In addition to support for the Pipeline Expansion, there was a significant and growing movement to acquire and become part of the pipeline ownership. Of the three groups interested, the earliest and most significant was the Western Indigenous Pipeline group, who represented the 55 First Nations along the pipeline route. They were looking at acquiring a 51% interest in the pipeline and the expansion project.

The group was led by Chief Michael LeBourdais of the Whispering Pines/Clinton Indigenous Band near Kamloops, British Columbia. He affirmed that the existing pipeline goes right through his reserve and they've never had major issues. He stated, "We're the ones most familiar with how the pipeline operates :we're the most familiar with the operations staff that are out here all the time." [80] He further expressed that pipelines generate solid revenue. He proudly stated that with revenue from this project, his band could build their own schools, hospitals and roads instead of being dependant on indigenous affairs government welfare.

Around this time, in spite of massive bureaucratic obstacles and perpetual judicial bickering, Kinder Morgan courageously confirmed a decision to move ahead with the Trans Mountain Expansion Project. This was a major step forward for the Canadian energy industry, taxpayers and indigenous people along the route.

On May 29, 2017, there was a big step backward as the BC NDP/Greens stole power from the Liberals. The NDP must rely on three Green MLAs for a single-seat majority over the governing Liberals. They illegally attempted to renege on then existing BC government

---

[80] Randy Shore, "First Nations Seek Influence in Trans Mountain Pipeline Purchase," *Vancouver Sun*, May 2019, https://vancouversun.com/news/local-news/first-nations-seek-influence-and-control-in-pipeline-purchase

approval. This would be regarded in most democratic rule of law societies as a blatant illegal breach of contract. Apparently not so here.

In October 2017, the pipeline builder asked the NEB to allow limited construction. This was allowed despite the objection of the city of Burnaby, who had no jurisdiction. In January 2018, the NEB performed another small step forward through the endless hoops and established a process to resolve permitting between the infrastructure builder municipalities and the provincial blockages.

In June 2018, the Supreme Court of British Columbia issued an injunction to block protestors from illegally disrupting the Trans Mountain construction site. This was to no avail, because it seemed to be a popular Vancouver Sunday afternoon recreation activity. A significant number of these protesters were paid by Greenpeace, Tides, Dogwood and other emotion-based environment activists. Some of these salaries actually traced back to the federal government. These were the instigators. Much of the mob knew little or nothing of the actual issues but simply felt good being part of a noble cause, however ill founded. Chaos, violence, illegal rioting and mob rule reigned supreme.

In April 2018, the pipeline developer Kinder Morgan finally stated the economically obvious: that it could not move forward forever with never-ending bureaucratic blockages, perpetual debates and continuing repetitive judicial meddling. It set a deadline of May 31, the beginning of construction season for the federal government, who approved the project to simply declare it in the national interest and have it move forward with no further impediments. That was within the power of the federal government. Kinder Morgan was done.

In May 2018, the federal government announced its intention to buy the pipeline and the proposed expansion for $4.5 billion.[81] Knowing the socialist tendencies of the Trudeau/Morneau Government, one wonders if that was not a background intention all along. For Canada, they would get it done. It was proclaimed as a monumental step essential to Canadian resource development. Problem solved. Except no.

In August 2018, the Federal Court of Appeal overturned the previous NEB and Trudeau government approval of the project. One has to comment at this point with the Trudeau future record for manipulation of the courts. One has to ask not only why this decision was not questioned but if it was actually politically sanctioned.

In September 2018, Natural Resources Minister Amarjeet Sohi ordered the NEB to redo its evaluation

---

[81] "Trans Mountain Timeline: A Look at the Key Dates in the Pipeline's History,"
https://www.bnnbloomberg.ca/trans-mountain-timeline-key-dates-in-the-history-of-the-pipeline.

of whales, tankers and indigenous consultation.[82] The NEB, with a panel of technical experts and qualified professionals, spent years reviewing this project. It was overturned by three local judges and a politician, none of which had any environmental, pipeline, marine or energy industry background. This launched another five months of delays as the NEB was given until February 2019 to redo and extend an already substantial report.

In October 2018, another hanger-on was brought in with the appointment of former Supreme Court Justice Frank Iacobucci[83] to repeat already completed indigenous consultations.

We again saw noble hypocrites in government, mainline churches and the left-wing media vehemently defending the indigenous rights of a very small, loud minority to say no. At the same time, they silently denied the rights of the vast majority of indigenous people and bands the right to say yes. They were being denied their basic opportunity to participate in today's economy.

In February 2019, the NEB presented yet another valid technical, professional report supporting the project. The federal government stated it would come back with a decision in May. In May, they stated they

---

[82] "Feds Give NEB 22 Weeks to Redo Trans Mountain Environmental Review," Canadian Press CTV News, September 2018, https://bc.ctvnews.ca/feds-give-neb-2eks-to-redo-trans-mountain-environmental-review.

[83] Kathleen Harris, "Ottawa Won't Appeal Trans Mountain Court Decision Appoints," *CBC News*, October 2018, https://www.cbc.ca/news/politics/sohi-trans-mountain-wednesday.

needed another month to make a decision they'd already made two years ago.

In June 2019, the Governor in Council directed the NEB to issue the certificate allowing the construction and operation of the Trans Mountain Expansion Project for the second time. The government statement was made that contracts to recruit staff and offer jobs could be made for September.[84] September was the end of the summer construction season. On September 4, 2019, the Federal Court of Appeal, playing a lesser game, stated it would dismiss some repetitive litigants such as municipalities. It nonetheless stated it would again hear from 6 out of 12 other litigants again.

For the third time, we were to review issues from indigenous groups, most of whom were not actually on the route. How many times can this go on?

Millions of taxpayer dollars for lawyers and bureaucrats were at stake. A basic statement by the government that it is in the national interest could have ended the court games charade. This particular Appeal Court statement did not override the June government statement allowing for preplanning for September. This preplanning was primarily limited to job recruitment and related contracts. The Liberal government twice approved the pipeline and bought it. The delays of recent months allowed the federal government to stall

---

[84] "How We Got There: Government of Canada Approves the Project," June 2019, https://www.transmountain.com/news/2019/how-we-got-here.

actual construction to go into the October 2019 federal election still sitting on the fence.

The pipeline was perceived to be a key issue in the October 2019 election. Without actual construction, protesters would be limited. Mr. Trudeau did not want vocal lower mainland protesters disrupting his re-election campaign. With construction approved, they thought supporters and economic realists could be conned into thinking something was happening. This way the government felt it can get support from both sides of the fence.

The bottom line is there have been seven years of study, debate, court cases and political approvals and rejections about this project. It cost billions of dollars in lost revenues and hundreds of millions in fees, all mostly unnecessary. The great Canadian approach put prosperity into peril.

Whether or not this issue affected the election one does not know. Strangely, despite their destruction of the Canadian energy industry, an uncontrolled, illegal immigration program and massive, escalating deficits, the Trudeau Liberal government was re-elected.

Limited work on actual construction of the Trans Mountain Project and the Burnaby Terminal finally commenced again in December 2019. One would hope the long-delayed, much-debated and overanalysed Trans Mountain Pipeline Expansion Project will move ahead. But construction of the pipeline will be on a phased approach. Every requirement must be checked off before each phase can begin. All condition filings must be approved on an ongoing basis by the NEB and a formal letter.

In January 2020, the Supreme Court of Canada unanimously rejected the Province of British Columbia's attempt to regulate the flow of crude oil and the Trans Mountain Pipeline Expansion.[85] The matter was federal jurisdiction. This was encouraging to Alberta and the pipeline proponent. In February 2020, the Supreme Court dismissed the remaining minor indigenous litigants. Finally!

Is the charade finished yet? It remains to be seen.
What Happened: Prosperity into Peril

- The original pipeline has produced oil safely since 1953.
- In 2012, Kinder Morgan announced an expansion plan.
- In 2012 The National Energy Board and Environmental Assessment Agencies conducted a study that consisted of four-plus years of expert evaluations, open hearings and indigenous consultations.
- In June 2016, Prime Justin Trudeau and federal government approved the project.

---

[85] Mia Rabson, "Supreme Court Rejects BC Appeal of Trans Mountain Pipeline Case," *Canadian Press Global News*, January 2020, https://globalnews.ca/news/6422235/supreme-court-bc-trans-mountain-appeal-rejected/.

- In 2016 Premier of BC Christy approved the project.
- In May 2017, municipalities and a few BC First Nations filed with Federal Appeal Court.
- In May 2017, New Horgan NDP/Green Provincial government reneged on BC approval.
- In April 2018, Kinder Morgan set the deadline for national interest declaration.
- In May 2018, the federal government bought the pipeline and expansion project.
- In August 2018, the Federal Court of Appeal overturned NEB and federal approval.
- 2018 Three unqualified judges and a politician overruled four years of expert evaluation.
- 2018 Another NEB review was ordered to readdress dealt-with issues.
- In June 2019, the project was re-recommended and ongoing planning was approved.
- In December 2019, with repeat approval, construction recommenced.
- In January 2020, the Supreme Court of Canada rejected BC opposition.

What Is Needed

- Create a step-by-step infrastructure evaluation process with published criteria done by qualified professionals.
- Decision to be respected

- Eliminate decision-making based on political whim.
- Abide by provincial jurisdiction of natural resources.
- Stop the use of the climate weapon to override resource jurisdiction.
- Project approval based on the specific project.
- End the use of hearings of repeated general concerns.
- Respect the right of indigenous people to say yes.

CHAPTER 11

Covid 19 Addendum

Earlier this year we addressed the problems encountered by the Canadian Industry and how productivity was being thwarted by endless government interference. Ways were pointed out as to how to get things back on track. WOW then we got hit with Covid 19. To many this was a problem to be addressed. To Canada's Federal Liberal government this was an opportunity. Firstly it would provide a smokescreen and a diversion to cover up their scandals and economic blundering. Secondly it would allow for shutting down significant portions of private business and replacing it with government handouts. My step by step economic recommendations were blown away. Control, control would not that be wonderful.

Public people to people interaction would occur only

where it was authorized . Banks would cease to deal with people except by computers, machines and internet. Much of their staff would be laid off. Doctors offices would be closed 90% closed. More staff and working people laid off. Prescriptions could be filled on a limited basis by pharmacists and/or telephone consultations. People with real medical problems, oh well tough luck.

Recreational facilities from swimming pools to gymnasiums. I like many seniors missed my aquasize classes. Retail outlets with the exception of grocery stores and liquor outlets would be closed for fear of public interaction. More people without paycheques. Factories were closed. Supply chains were interrupted such that farmers could not market their foodstuffs while grocery stores went without products. More economic loss! Bars and restaurants were closed or severely limited. More lost paycheques and private business hardship. Airline travel and vacation entities closed or very very limited. Advanced travel plan deposits gone. Airlines with leased aircraft and no revenue on the brink of collapse. More lost wages and income. Prices for raw materials collapse resulting in reduced pricing and production. More business and personal loss. Schools were closed causing more social instability and collapse. Measures were certainly necessary. This was an international virus that had ravaged and spread across the world. Hand sanitizers a reasonable defense. Visitor controls on Senior homes where the risk was higher definitely needed. Border controls and flight restrictions were merited. Continued influx of unregulated illegal refugees from countries with major medical issues was total absurdity. I am not an epidemiologist but common sense would dictate that measures were more political than medical. Fallout from the shutdown has far exceeded the consequences of a virus with a very high recovery rate. Vestiges of a police state. Suicides and drug overdose deaths are frightening.

Not to worry our wonderful socialist and the ever concerned Mr Trudeau would step in and save the day. The Canadian Emergency Response Benefit (CERB) would be his gift to Canada from other people's money. CERB the great economic impetus. From mid March to mid August 2020 with this program the government would dole out $69.4 billion dollars to 4.1 million people. That is $8,061 per person. Millions of Canadians did not receive that kind of money when they and the economy were working.

During this time the economy was generating only sharply reduced revenue and hence much reduced taxes. Dollar in dollar out in the cold light of dawn they have to eventually match. The Canadian Liberal Federal government debt would soar to over a trillion dollars. So let's look at how these funds were doled out. If you were eligible you received $500 per week ie $2000 per month for four weeks . You were eligible to re-apply for 28 weeks. That is absolute madness that involves flagrant government handouts that are not sustainable.

To qualify you had to have earned in the previous year $5000 from employment income, self employment or provincial benefits related to maternity benefits. So you made $5000, in the last year and the government is going to pay you $2000per month in emergency income substitution????? Good God figure that one. So I digress. Stipulated is that if your work hours have been reduced by the Covid 19 shutdown or are unable to work or have stopped working because of Covid 19 or if because of Covid 19 you are taking care of someone. Give me a break regular care workers don't necessarily normally make $2000 per month. Certainly people had to eat, support their families and make rent or mortgage payments. A speed up and expansion of the Employment Insurance program could have accomplished this. But no the socialist Mr Trudeau had to make it a gift from him and the government. Had to make it a further dependence on government and weaken private sector employment. Satisfying his ego gave billions in payments to those both not affected by and affected by Covid shutdown job loss.

What are we now looking at as some of the Covid shutdown restrictions are relaxed and employment opportunities begin to open back up? Do people want to go back to work or do they continue to collect the $2000 per month Covid freebie. Most people would prefer to work but not all. With the Covid idleness the work ethic has been reduced, motivation has been reduced. Domestic violence, , suicide, alcohol abuse and drug overdose deaths have all increased. Government dependency is triumphing. To the further weakening of our society some businesses and their owners have moved from viable entities to government handouts. The socialist government has used the Covid situation to weaken the Free Enterprise economy and increase government dependency. This is not healthy but before I go on to further discuss the socioeconomic cost of Covid and the Covid shutdown I will discuss student benefits.

The Canada Emergency Student Benefit (CESB) was designed to provide financial support to post-secondary students and recent post-secondary and high school graduates who were unable to find work do to Covid 19 and the Covid 19 shutdown. From May to August 2020 the program provided for those eligible $1250 for each four week period or $2000 for each 4 week period if you had dependents or a disability. Well I think a lot of students, professional students and potential students could document dependents. Again we are seeing the great socialist myth. You do not have to try the government will support you. There is no point in saving for an education. There is no advantage to personal initiative Mr Trudeau will grant all if you fill out the government paperwork.

More stuff here we go. Canada Emergency Business Account (CEBA) will provide interest free loans of up to $40,000 to small businesses and not-for-profits with 25% being forgivable. Note the latter this can be claimed by churches, mosques or any supposed charitable cause. Entities without public support or justifiable need are suddenly on the government payroll.

The Canadian Emergency Wage Subsidy (CEWS). CEWS applies at a rate of 75% of the first $58,700 normally earned by an employee. This represents a benefit of up to $847 per week, per employee. This is wildly open to fudged figures and fraud. Could apply to salaries that were never in jeopardy. Government salaries? The Canadian Commercial Rent Assistance will provide to commercial property owners a forgivable loan for rent reduction of at least 75% to businesses who experience a 70% drop from pre-Covid revenues. Again another supposedly virtuous concept open to fraud and encouraging government dependency. Where did all the bureaucrats to regulate these programs come from . How much were they paid. Did they have any qualifications. Or more likely in reality there was no control. NO,NO,NO to all of this, we cannot afford it. And the debt zoomed up.

It has to stop. The push forward by many is opposite. Recardo Tranjan of the Canadian Centre for Policy Alternatives is advocating for these type of things to be permanent parts of a social safety net. Jagmeet Singh and the socialist NDP have granted support to the Liberal minority government for going with these concepts. The virtue signalling is working . Sadly the realty is support to government friends and chosen entities as opposed to viable businesses and enterprises. The government is further trying to tie free enterprise to their apron strings. There is a cost both bureaucratic and real to all of this. It will have to come from taxing individuals and business. This will be a drag on recovery for both those who played the game and those who did not.

These Covid 19 shut down expenditures are being paid for by massive deficits and exploding debt. There will be a push for higher taxes. The fiscal platform from former Finance Minister Morneau is frightening. The deficit for 2020-21 will rise to $343 billion. The net federal debt will hit $1.2 Trillion $1,200,000,000. That is twelve hundred billion or $33,300 for every man, woman and child in the Country. The really scary thing is that this Finance Minister was replaced because he would not spend more. We need less government not more. The governments will eventually have to realize that business and industry have been weakened by all that has gone on and revenue generation will be lower and slow to come back. Many businesses especially in retail will never come back. Prime Minister Justin Trudeau and new Finance Minister Christia Freeland cannot or do not care to address this. With the current American election this poisonous attitude of government handouts with no sense of economic reality seems to have even extended south to the United States.

Municipal governments in places such as Toronto, Vancouver and Calgary also seem to be at fault. Calgary Mayor Naheed Nenshi has shifted tax losses from the downtown failed oil and gas industry onto already suffering local adjacent businesses rather than making necessary spending cuts. Those already suffering from the energy industry downturn were whacked with harsher than needed Covid restrictions. Mayor John Tory of Toronto attacks local restaurants and bars. The Vancouver mayor focuses on "greenie" theories as opposed to reality. We have to get our businesses and industry back. The government has to reduce not expand it's emphasis on costly ineffective "Green" energy. Did they not watch Michael Moore's move "Planet of the Humans ". His factual portrayal of the misplaced economics and failure of wind, solar and biofuels is indisputable. Government has to retreat and let Free Enterprise rebuild the economy on proven energy resources or we face a vastly devalued Canadian dollar and socio-economic disaster. With the 2020 election propaganda sadly our American neighbours once the world pillar of democracy could be heading the same direction.

So time marches on and we have in Canada a throne speech that fortunately did not contain the total socialization of the Canadian Economy as feared. It did contain however the making permanent of the unregulated CERB handouts. As of Sept 26, 2020 the CERB was replaced by the more permanent Canada Recovery Benefit (CRB) . It will again be $2000 per month for up to 26 weeks for those who can claim employment loss due to Covid 19 shutdowns and are not eligible for Employment Insurance programs. There will also be CRSB a Canada Recovery Caregiving Benefit of $500 per week for 26 weeks if you can claim caring for a child or other dependent. The madness becomes permanent. No filtering, no incentive to work and punishment for those who try. These measures were going to be put before the electorate. But our second great socialist party the NDP led by Mr Singh voted with the government on the condition that his even more radical destructive policies be included. My solid step by step recommendations for a better free enterprise approach to resource development and prosperity are swamped away by this socialist madness. A United Nations concept of world socialist government induced by fear is not the answer to Canadian or American post Covid recovery.

We are now being told of the coming "Great Reset". One dreads to think.

CONCLUDING REMARKS

Canada is a great nation with good people and large potential. It is a vast country with large cities and immense resources. We built a railroad through the wilderness for 8,000 kilometres from the Atlantic Ocean to the Pacific Ocean. We have a vast highway network from the Pacific to the Arctic to the Atlantic. We currently are stalled and going 'round and 'round in circles. Our evaluation system for major development projects was once a step-by-step process with stipulated parameters run by qualified technical and professional experts. It has been replaced by decisions made on political whim. We have been bogged down by supposed noble ideas that are really about shifting power to Ottawa. They increase bureaucracy. They do not enhance our society. They lessen productivity. They, along with the stalling and rejection of infrastructure projects, have put our prosperity into peril. A powerful central government has deliberately overwhelmed the regions to the point of potential breakup. Our democratic process has been disrupted by a judicial system that has the power to stall, repeat and go nowhere. Major efforts and investment subsequently fall off the table. A single segment of the country, often referred to as the old-money Laurentian elite, has disproportionate power. A unproductive, unregulated, heavily subsidized influx of foreign entities is flooding our culture. Government institutions, departments and agencies that should be politically neutral no longer seem to be. Our universities and colleges seem to be more interested in socialist dogma than educating young people for needed vocations.

If these issues can be resolved, we will once again be a great nation with an exceptional future.

Today, our prosperity is in peril and Canada in Chaos.

BIBLIOGRAPHY

Ball, Tim. *The Deliberate Corruption of Climate Science.* Apache Junction, AZ: Stairway Press, 2014.

Benstead, Walter, 1982, Petroleum and Potash Potential of Southwest Manitoba Indian Reserves, prepared for the Dakota Ojibway Tribal Council and Indian Affairs Benstead, Walter, 2014, Permian Brachiopods of Melville Island, Canadian Arctic, compared to Svalbard, Norway, in Alberta Palaeontological 18th Annual Symposium

Benstead, Walter 2014, Popular Geology of the Panorama Ski Hill, Wings over the Rockies Symposium.

Drummond, K. J. Future Petroleum Provinces of Canada, Their Geology and Potential—Memoir 1, 1973. Canadian Society of Petroleum Geologists.

Hart, Michael. *Hubris: The Troubling Science, Economics and Politics of Climate Change.* Ottawa, Canada: Compleat Desktops Publishing, 2015.

Laframboise, Donna. *The Delinquent Teenager Who Was Mistaken for the World's Top Climate Expert: IPPC Expose.* Toronto: Ivy Avenue Press, 2011.

Levant, Ezra. *Trumping Trudeau: How Donald Trump Will Change Canada Even If Justin Trudeau Doesn't Know It Yet.* Rebel Media Network, 2017.

Levant, Ezra. The Libranos Rebel Media Network 2019

Lomborg, Bjorn. *The Skeptical Environmentalist: Measuring the Real State of the World.* Cambridge University Press, 2001.

Moore, Patrick. *Confessions of a Greenpeace Dropout: The Making of a Sensible Environmentalist.* Vancouver: Beatty Street Publishing Inc., 2010.

Wiskel, Bruno. *The Emperor's New Climate: Debunking the Myths of Global Warming.* Evergreen Environmental Company Ltd., 2006.

Wrightson, Gregory. *Inconvenient Facts: The Science That Al Gore Doesn't Want You to Know.* Silver Crown Productions, 2017.

www.ingramcontent.com/pod-product-compliance
Lightning Source LLC
Chambersburg PA
CBHW021426070526
44577CB00001B/85